Architecture of Skidmore, Owings & Merrill, 1963–1973

Architecture of Skidmore, Owings & Merrill, 1963–1973

Introduction by Arthur Drexler
Commentaries by Axel Menges

The Monacelli Press

Copyright © 1974 by Skidmore, Owings & Merrill LLP

All rights reserved. Published in the United States by The Monacelli Press,
a division of Random House, Inc., New York

Originally published in a bilingual edition in Germany by Verlag Gerd Hatje, Stuttgart, and in the
United States by Architectural Book Publishing Co., Inc., New York, in 1974.

The Monacelli Press is a trademark of Random House, Inc.

Library of Congress Cataloging-in-Publication Data
Skidmore, Owings & Merrill.
SOM : architecture of Skidmore, Owings & Merrill, 1963–1973 / introduction by Arthur Drexler ;
commentaries by Axel Menges. — 1st ed.
p. cm.
Originally published: Architecture of Skidmore, Owings & Merrill, 1963–1973. Bilingual ed.
Stuttgart, Germany : Verlag Gerd Hatje, 1974 and New York : Architectural Book Pub. Co., 1974.
ISBN 978-1-58093-221-9
1. Skidmore, Owings & Merrill. 2. Architecture—United States—History—20th century. I. Menges,
Axel. II. Title. III. Title: Architecture of Skidmore, Owings & Merrill, 1963–1973.
NA737.S53A4 2009b
720.92'2—dc22   2009009234

Printed in China

www.monacellipress.com

10 9 8 7 6 5 4 3 2 1
First Monacelli Press edition

Project Editors: Elizabeth Harrison Kubany and Landis Livingston Carey

Jacket design: Pentagram Design Inc.
With acknowledgment to Chermayeff & Geismar

Contents

Introduction

What is called modern architecture has now survived more social upheavals, transformed more of the built environment, and established hegemony over more disparate cultures than any architectural manifestation of the Western world since the Roman Empire. Roman in its claim to universality, the international style, like science, is practiced and understood everywhere. Merely to be Chinese or Russian or African is no excuse for mismanaging its techniques and configurations. There is no other way to build.

A style that began under the aegis of utilitarianism, invoking economy of means along with a taste for "simplicity," now embraces extravagance as well as poverty. The rich, like the poor, cannot escape modernism; even wealth must pretend to prudent "solutions" to "problems." The movement abounds in masterpieces, but these are seldom considered to be the product of private inspiration, essentially incommunicable. At all levels of accomplishment excellence is understood to be the result of right practice, which can be taught; those who have learned it can work together and we may expect continuous improvement. Experience confirms the theory – or at least does not disprove it. Why then has modern architecture lost so much of its original coherence? Why has the certainty that once struck with the force of revelation turned first to uneasy iconoclasm and, lately, to a nervous ecumenism? More awkward still: how is it possible for an international movement of such magnitude to have reached its present age without serious philosophical probing of its fundamental assumptions?

Any answer must begin with the fact of success: modernism prevails, and must now take responsibility for the ills its exponents claimed it could overcome. These ills were not diagnosed as afflictions of the aesthetic sense, except as poor vision might be considered a side effect of cancer. They were held to be the result of society's unwillingness, or inability, to fairly distribute and intelligently use the wealth made possible by industrialization. Therefore every solution to an architectural problem was expected to serve as a prototype, a model for the eventual reconstruction of the village, the city, the world. But the notion that architecture is a suitable instrument for effecting social reform is as foolish now as it has always been. Architects are servants, not masters, and like all good servants they can persuade their masters to modify bad habits whenever it makes no serious difference. Unlike other servants, however, they will be blamed for their masters' failings.

For those who await the revolution from moment to moment, what provokes unease is not the success of individual architectural achievements but rather their appropriation by the very people whose lives such good works were supposed to transform. The oppressors continue to oppress, only now they do so from headquarters whose good design was meant to be morally redeeming. To this indignity we may add the disgrace of a social apparatus incapable of coping, at least in the United States, with the most urgent and obvious problems – housing, for example, and transportation.

Despite the servitude of architects, economic and social factors are not the sole determinants of built urban form; the will of the architect and the dogma of modern architecture have played their part. Bromidic as the Marxist complaint about formalism may be, it does take account of a phenomenon which, at the same time, it fails to explain: the architect's will to make form can and does impose itself on society, sometimes with disastrous effect, sometimes with saving grace. Our judgements of quality, inseparable from our notions of what is desirable, continue to be predicated on ideas about architecture, technology, economics and social well-being that have their origin in circumstances we no longer find humanly acceptable. Yet with or without a re-examination of theories and assumptions, the formal possibilities of the new architecture continue to unfold. Not every interesting possibility has been tried; the store of useful ideas is by no means exhausted, and already much that was rejected, or undervalued, at the beginning of the movement is being re-integrated in a more generous perspective. (The process starts with neglected Italian work of the 'thirties and will no doubt soon reach its counterparts in Austria, Czechoslovakia, and Hungary.)

There is another body of neglected work, even harder to see whole. It constitutes current normative practice and seldom engages in the polemics that are thought to make up architectural history. Perhaps that alone is sufficient reason to examine the work of the most able practitioners, as distinguished from the few initiating geniuses. Several candidates are eligible for such consideration; none more so than Skidmore, Owings and Merrill. For more than 35 years in the United States, and since World War II in other countries as well, the firm has tested the viability of most assumptions of the modern movement.

SOM comprises approximately 1,000 architects, engineers and technicians. From within the firm they are able to provide complete services in planning, designing, engineering and construction supervision. Seven principal offices – New York, Chicago, San Francisco, Portland, Oreg., Washington, D.C., Paris, and Los Angeles – are directed by twenty-five general partners. Working arrangements on a given project, headed by a partner in charge of design, vary from the close association of colleagues to the execution of design decisions made by one man. The firm's commissions range from the exotic – a Presidential library, for example – to such more or less routine matters as industrial or transportation facilities; whether they are conspicuous or recessive all of these buildings receive an attention to detail vital to the philosophy and ethics of modern architecture. In this connection Bruce Graham of the Chicago office relates a significant story. Faced with having to design a hospital, he remarked to Mies van der Rohe that it presented endless technical problems and little opportunity for the pleasures of architecture. To this, according to Graham, Mies responded: "*I do not have to design such buildings, but you must.*" It is indeed the compulsion to solve the least rewarding problems, as well as the most interesting, that has given SOM its enviable reputation.

Publishing house and printing plant of the newspaper "The Republic," Columbus, Indiana.

Once praised for the consistent quality and character of its work, then sometimes criticized for being too consistent, SOM's recent practice often draws simultaneous praise and blame – to the same building – for the consistent quality of its innovations. The present variety may be a product of those accidents of temperament and personal inclination which so often determine the character of large enterprises. Certainly some of it reflects, if it is not actually caused by, a more willing acceptance of the fact that responsibility for buildings ultimately rests on individuals. Each of them has a name, and where twenty years ago the firm was reluctant to identify individual members, it does so now as a matter of course.

SOM no longer has a single house style – it never really did – but it does have distinct regional habits. The difference between the Chicago and the New York office is conspicuous; both offices differ even more from the San Francisco approach, and within each of these three main divisions there are individual variations. The most important of these is undoubtedly the direction taken by Walter Netsch in Chicago, setting aside the organization of buildings according to their structural systems in favor of complex plan geometries. Netsch's preoccupation with geometry also has roots in Chicago through Frank Lloyd Wright, yet in the present American architectural scene one might have expected this idea to have been pursued on the West Coast; certainly the San Francisco office is more relaxed about the management of structure.

The Chicago office has distinguished itself by developing several structural systems more efficient for highrise towers. Some of these continue in the direction inaugurated – or at least clarified – by Mies van der Rohe, and insofar as there may be a center of gravity, a continuity that by now takes on the character of tradition, it is the relatively constant Chicago preoccupation with buildings that are structurally "tough." To the extent that they have themselves done more to enlarge the scope of this tradition than any other architects in the United States, SOM's Chicago office may be said to stand at the center of American practice. Yet it is in New York that some of these ideas have been given interpretations no less forceful, and certainly more surprising, than in Chicago. The notion of minimal form as skin rather than bones, for example, reaches its apogee in New York with Gordon Bunshaft's Marine Midland Building at 140 Broadway. The expressive power of massive steel framing is carried to what might seem to be its logical conclusion not in Bruce Graham's John Hancock Center in Chicago, but in Roy Allen's U.S. Steel building in New York. And although its point of departure is structural efficiency, Bruce Graham's Sears Tower in Chicago is of still greater interest for solving a visual rather than a structural problem: its massing as a set of towers of uneven height reduces apparent bulk and restores a more varied skyline – the kind of problem that might have been expected to attract the attention of architects in New York. And again, it is not Walter Netsch's penchant for the more emotionally subtle response, or Bruce Graham's and Fazlur Khan's for the technically sophisticated, that has yielded SOM's few exercises in architecture as part of an organic "ecological" whole, but rather Edward Bassett's Weyerhaeuser building near Tacoma and Gordon Bunshaft's office complex for the American Can Company near New York, both on suburban meadowland and both concerned with enhancing their sites.

In some way that probably cannot be demonstrated, SOM's work is a dialogue between its regional offices. Regional distinctions alone, however, provide no adequate framework for evaluation. It would seem more logical to consider SOM's work according to building types, as in fact they have been grouped in this book. Useful enough for purposes of comparison, analysis by building type merely reveals that there are four or five ways to generate variations on the same type; the subdivisions are so numerous as to render analysis by function as misleading as analysis by structure. What seems inescapable is analysis according to intent. That this may require mind reading, as well as a certain skepticism toward what is avowed, should not obscure the fact that intent is often enough self-evident – more often, indeed, than structural systems or building programs.

Structure and materials at one level, detail and integrating composition at another, are the means with which intent is signified.

Even though it has been largely rejected during the last decade, the idea that architecture can be produced with structure alone has had an authority that is still all-pervading. The structural motif continues to signify the attitude of responsibility, like a business suit or a briefcase or whatever other accoutrement may be selected to indicate a fixed position near the top of a hierarchy. The structural systems that constitute accepted form language for this emotional message have of course been established by Ludwig Mies van der Rohe. To Mies structure meant one material: steel. His concern was to develop an absolute structure whose logical validity would transcend any particular condition of site or program. He defined the ideal building as a one-story pavilion with a flat, clear-span roof, coffered because the equal distribution of stresses justifies the equal distribution of perimeter columns on identical elevations. But the intent is not structural clarity for its own sake. It is rather to respond to the contingent world with a sobriety that can withstand or evade the unexpected. There is no inherent reason why structure in steel, or any other material, must be deployed to signify sobriety, and although the mood, the material and the forms have together dominated consciousness for so long that they now seem inseparable, and are characteristic of much of SOM's work as of everyone else's, there are obvious alternatives. Structure can be used to signify frivolity, if that is the opposite of sobriety, and all shades of deportment in between.

Removed from sobriety but not yet frivolous is the one-story office and printing plant designed for the newspaper "The Republic" in Columbus, Indiana, by Myron Goldsmith. A long, rectangular block, with columns evenly spaced on all sides, it signifies its mood by the thinness of its structural members: here we do what we have to, neither apologizing nor explaining. Thus the square bays are not expressed on the perimeter, where closely spaced columns each carry slim I beams to the larger central spans. Box-like lighting fixtures under a ribbed ceiling complete the range of structural detail, so that the assemblage of component parts tends to look manufactured rather than built. Two relatively subjective design decisions are allowed: first, glazing is divided into two lights of identical height, the upper section treated as an opaque plane concealing the column structure on the end elevations. Second: the steel is painted white, a color Mies reserved for the relaxations of the countryside. The effect is calm, insistent but not compulsive, and with a vague affinity for the thin-walled boxes of Japanese architecture in its abrupt change from solid to void at the corners. What is less relaxing is that only by keeping his eyes on the ground can the visitor hope to find his way to the entrance; the elevations offer no clue, and the plan provides no more than an orderly containment of necessary spaces.

Nothing in this building's program requires that a visit to it should constitute a momentous event in someone's life. Architecture like this – and it is Architecture, not building – rejects more opportunities to amuse than it accepts. That is not the case as one moves toward the other end of the emotional scale for which structure is the significant form.

Two examples that bring home the point are the central engineering building for Armstrong Cork, by Roy Allen, and the office building for the Boots Company by Bruce Graham. Both buildings emphasize the roof plate as a massive horizontal plane, justified at Armstrong by using it to accommodate mechanical equipment; both set glass walls behind their perimeter columns; and both accommodate a lower floor as a subordinate element, almost concealed for Boots (where it is expressed as a base or pedestal related to the ground plane rather than the columns) and articulated at Armstrong where the top floor reads as a *piano nobile*.

The Boots building makes use of square bays in a classic 3 to 5 ratio, its evenly stressed elevations concealing the fact that the main internal feature of the building is a sunk garden to which both floors open. The rectangular structural bays of the Armstrong building, in a ratio of 4 to 16, provide a more insistent rhythm in the long elevations, but on the narrow ends the perimeter columns are eliminated for the upper floor, so that the roof plate

Central engineering building of the Armstrong Cork Company, Lancaster, Pennsylvania.

Headquarters of the Boots Pure Drug Company, Nottingham, England.

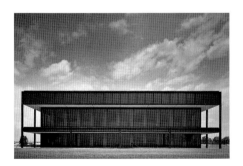

appears to be a clear span. On neither building is structure modified for any purpose; only the approach road, for example, can find the door, which is otherwise unaccented, yet the cage-like character of the structure is contradicted by its tactical impenetrability.

Both of these buildings are pavilion types widely used by SOM for a variety of purposes. The type derives from Mies' School of Architecture and Design at Illinois Institute of Technology, with its thin roof plate suspended from enormous trusses to provide uninterrupted loft space for a *piano nobile*, and a basement floor whose actual means of support is in no way visible from the elevations but is in fact a normal distribution of interior columns (as is the case with the Boots building). The ambiguities inherent in this parti have been variously resolved by minimizing the difference in structural treatment or by implying that the lower floor is in some way a separate structure related to the ground plane. However it is treated, the main force of the design depends on the visual plausibility of the structure as column-and-roof. Suppression or emphasis of detail becomes particularly important. Thus, stiffening flanges on both Boots and Armstrong help to place the buildings in the realm of engineering; the rigorous expression of a module in all interior fittings sustains the aura of inevitability; the choice of exterior color – dark – sustains the mood of earnest endeavor. And although the programs for such buildings seldom demand the articulation of some particular feature, neither do they demand equalization within a single rectangular container. The real advantage is that extended, regular elevations suggest that there is no rational alternative, and offer a structural system in such abundance that, if there were less of it, its muscularity might seem somewhat exaggerated. Yet in both buildings the Miesian objective of craft and purity is achieved in fact as well as in fancy. From mechanical equipment to furniture, interior fittings are pleasingly if relentlessly integrated. At all scales the precision of detail is beautiful. Yet the result is curiously frustrating, perhaps because the energy, persistence and intelligence brought to bear on structural detail cannot be related to any purpose other than their own. The dilemma is fundamental to "rational" architecture.

The expressive range indicated for these three structures by no means indicates the gamut; it does suggest the plausible limits for low, moderately large structures of essentially utilitarian character. A change in scale from low horizontal building to vertical slab or tower obviously increases the opportunities for structural invention, and it may be useful to consider first what may be the SOM skyscraper equivalent to Myron Goldsmith's "The Republic" building. In the context of the work included in this book, that equivalent is the 19-story Business Men's Assurance Co. office building in Kansas City. It is quite simply an unadorned structural cage, a rectangle in plan of three to five bays, all square, standing on a low paved platform. A slight, almost imperceptible increase in height differentiates the ground floor arcade from the rest of the structure; columns and beams are of the same dimension and the glass wall is set well back so that the cage stands free and clear. In a sense this is the archetypal skeleton structure, abstracted of all superfluous detail and apparently capable of receiving whatever one chooses to put inside it, given the limits of the 36′ bays. Since it stands alone in a park, and since its frame is clad with white marble whose slight grain is invisible at a distance, it seems like an abstract architectural model that happens to have been built full scale. Considering that the formal idea has precedent in Giuseppe Terragni's Casa del Fascio, built at Como in 1932, and was subsequently elaborated by Terragni and others in the years just prior to World War II, it is surprising that it had to wait until the mid-60's before anyone actually built it in the United States. Terragni's Casa del Fascio explored the ambiguities that result from articulating a rectangular column and beam structure and, in the same wall plane, leaving it undifferentiated from a solid infill. The contradiction between structure and non-structure was reinforced by a uniform veneer of white stucco; the white marble cladding used in the Business Men's Assurance building serves the same purpose of abstracting the form so that it ceases to look "built" (although joints and marble veining are a minor distraction). But between the Italian manipulation of column and wall, and the Business Men's Assurance building stands Mies van der Rohe. What we have now is a structure purified by suppressing the wall and abstracting the structure itself. Beyond that, design decisions consist essentially in the elimination of detail, or at least in making detail unobtrusive, and the building carries no particular emotional tone. On the other hand, although it is not exactly lighthearted, it can only make its point by avoiding the portentous accents of engineering. Indeed, it comes amazingly close to being just what it looks like: a rudimentary skeleton structure.

Headquarters of the Business Men's Assurance Co. of America, Kansas City, Missouri.

Tenneco Building, Houston, Texas.

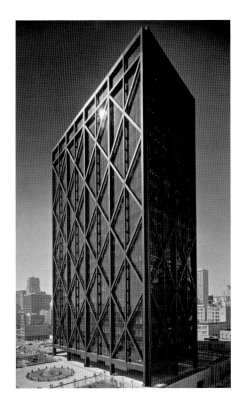

Alcoa Building, San Francisco, California.

John Hancock Center, Chicago, Illinois.

What happens when the same theme does take on structural detail can be seen in the Tenneco building. Though substantially larger – 33 stories, seven bays to each side with interior columns replaced by central utility cores – Tenneco is nevertheless the same structural cage with recessed glass walls. Here, however, the cage is articulated. Columns are pulled slightly forward to stress the vertical line; the street level arcade is three stories high; the columns receive an extra "buttress" up to the middle of the first fascia; and a horizontal sun shade hangs from each floor like an upside down parapet. Dark metal cladding helps to suggest that these details are derived from structural considerations. The result is without the abstract, nearly scaleless quality of the Business Men's Assurance building, nor is it yet so engineered as to seem like more effort than the problem requires.

The Tenneco building takes form derived from "minimum" structure to something just short of the mid-point of its expressive possibilities; beyond this the form derives either from improved structural efficiency or from some other quality implicit in the building as a whole. Lightness and grace, or horizontal stacks of floors, or verticality, for example, are all available for expressive elaboration, but what tends to be selected for emphasis is the idea of massive power, strength, and weight, characteristics which are not necessarily in the spirit of a developing technology of light, efficient, high-rise construction. An example is the United States Steel building in New York at 1 Liberty Plaza, which in fact does achieve a remarkable economy of materials despite its massive appearance, but before considering its formal implications it may be more useful to review the SOM structural innovations that seem to indicate the future of skyscraper design.

It is not necessary to recapitulate in detail the variations, which begin with the introduction of larger spans and evolve in relation to the demand for greater height at a reasonable cost. The main line of development has, of course, been concerned with the problem of stabilizing structure, and has focused attention on the contradiction between an expressed orthogonal frame and the lateral bracing normally concealed within core walls. Precedent for expressing the diagonal has been variously cited as going back to the Eames House of 1949, the Crystal Palace of 1851, or the buttressing of gothic cathedrals. It would be conceded that the truss walls of Mies' Convention Hall project of 1953 revealed some of the design possibilities of expressed lateral framing, although it is sometimes forgotten that Mies first explored the idea in 1934, with a project for a glasswalled house cantilevered from a hillside. In skyscraper design, however, Mies continued to reject expressed lateral framing. Like Japanese architects of the classical period, he apparently regarded such framing as something to be concealed at all costs. Psychologically the attitude is akin to that of the Greeks in the Hellenistic period; they understood quite well the principle of the arch but preferred to reserve such excessively dynamic construction for sewers. As the distinction between the art of architecture and the science of engineering has blurred, that attitude is no longer psychologically persuasive. But the first experiments with this technique are cast in the language of engineering, not "art" – the distinction is still operative. One result is that the idea seems at first sight grotesquely in excess of what is required, despite its demonstrable economic advantages. Thus SOM's San Francisco office rejected a 1957 study for a building with expressed lateral framing because it was only 17 stories high, and not until the 27-story Alcoa building of 1967 was there a suitable occasion to try it out. Interesting as the Alcoa building may be, it too seems not quite big enough to justify its structure and the attendant, albeit minor, inconveniences to the building's occupants, whose views out are interrupted by unintelligible fragments flying across the windows.

The first suitable opportunity occurred with the 100-story John Hancock Center of 1970. This combines accommodations in one massive, tapered, rectangular tower for department stores on the ground, third and fourth floors; parking from the sixth to the twelfth floors; offices from the thirteenth to the forty-first floors; apartments from the forty-sixth to the ninety-second floors; and restaurant-observation level, TV studio and mechanical space above. These are incorporated in a structure and a height module that in no way differentiates their diverse functions. In the apartments the sloping perimeter walls and massive beams and columns, including the slanting ones, produce an effect not unlike that of a renovated garret in Berlin or Paris, although the distractions of obtrusive structure are compensated by spectacular views, if not by garret rents.

Seen from the other side of Chicago the tapered profile of the Hancock building is an extraordinarily compelling urban image. As one approaches the building, catching glimpses of it in the kaleidoscope of urban forms, and as its detail becomes visible, its mesmerizing effect increases. Approaching it at ground level, close up, introduces a rude shock: this gigantic construction stands on a one-story travertine pedestal, as if it were a paperweight. All striving to express the dynamics of a maximally efficient structure ends abruptly some twelve feet above ground level. The solidity implied by a stone base is disrupted by shop windows and minimal entrances, compounding the confusion. The contrast between a very low entrance and a massive superstructure may of course be used to advantage, and is not problematic in itself. But mediating between the scale of the street and the scale of the building is certainly one of the functions of an entrance; it is a function that architects around the world have grappled with but have rarely solved with complete success in the urban high-rise context. SOM's intelligence has not yet been applied to the problem with anything like the energy concentrated on solving structural problems. In the John Hancock Center, where engineering ends it is improvisation, not architecture, that takes over.

Another Chicago structural exercise seems to hold more intrinsic architectural significance: the 109-story Sears Tower. The theme is essentially a building made up of buildings: nine towers packed in a square rise to different heights. Each tower is 75 feet square and each is a structural tube whose clear spans are framed by perimeter columns spaced six to a side, including the shared corner columns which are of larger dimension. During construction an extraordinary and beautiful space sequence is revealed in looking from one tower into the others; on completion, of course, office partitions will obliterate this internal clarity. But the unquestioned structural efficiency and economy of the Sears Tower, while it may be the only justification necessary to its brilliant engineer, is not itself the most interesting aspect. The form is doubly persuasive precisely because it can be built with other structural systems. The clear articulation of component towers equal in all dimensions except their height provides what now seems an obvious solution to several problems at once. It suggests possible ways of differentiating functions for buildings intended to accommodate so-called "24 hour" programs, such as the John Hancock. It suggests ways in which the composition of a tower can be made more responsive to its immediate environment, since its component parts can be oriented to advance or recede in relation to what goes on around them. And finally it suggests that height expressed through dominantly vertical detail might perhaps take second place to height expressed through massing itself – the building affords pure vertical ascent for each of its parts with the advantages of set-backs in its totality. What is left to refine is the articulation of the skin, and most particularly the treatment of the column where one tower stops and the adjacent tower continues upward. Perhaps because the formal idea came first, and a suitable structure was applied to it, the Sears Tower can be experienced as technique in the service of form rather than the other way around. It is difficult to think of another skyscraper put up in the United States during the last 15 years that opens up as many possibilities of form and structure alike.

If the Hancock building casts architecture in the idiom of civil engineering, and if the Sears building rationalizes towers of varying heights by a suitable structural technique, the 54-story tower for U.S. Steel, at 1 Liberty Plaza in New York, occupies a more ambiguous territory. Here the intent is to use steel as visibly and assertively as possible: it is what the client sells. Initial studies were directed toward the use of plate steel to make a bearing wall, but the time required for research and legal clearances ruled it out in favor of what is essentially a conventional skeleton frame with a stabilizing core. The significant innovation is that greater stress loads are carried on the perimeter, through spandrel girders whose great depth allows reduction of the web to a thickness of ¼": Besides reducing the role of a stabilizing core, there is an additional economy in taking care of one half of the skin with the steel structure itself.

The U.S. Steel tower is a rectangle with a bay ratio of three to five. These bays are 50 feet on the long elevations, with the dimension increased almost imperceptibly on the narrow ends (where the central bay is wider still). The 6'3" height of the spandrel girders equals the height of the windows, and is enough to absorb the suspended ceiling as well as the parapet and heating element on the floor above. Because the webs of each of the spandrel girders are not fireproofed on the outside, their flanges have been extended (over a core of sprayed-on fireproofing material) to act as a flame shield. With the addition of these shields the total setback for the glass is more than two feet, so that the bottom flange acts as a sunshade.

Columns, however, are conventionally fireproofed and steel-clad. With the flange of each column articulated as an element slightly more than one foot wide, the actual column face is made to read as an unusually wide reveal. Spandrels and columns are thus part of the

Sears Tower, Chicago, Illinois.

U.S. Steel Building, New York, New York.

Marine Midland Building, New York, New York.

same grammar of steel girder construction, brought up to a scale normally associated with elevated highways or railroad crossings and contradicted by every building in the vicinity. The immediate visual impression is that if the U.S. Steel building is structurally sound, then everything around it must be unsafe; if the others are safe, then the U.S. Steel building must be something of an exaggeration. The sheer quantity of metal displayed to the eye is perhaps no more than would be consumed by dividing the structural bays with closely spaced vertical mullions, or using some other cladding system; it is, of course, the reversal of proportions between solid and void that makes the difference. This is not a glass building with a skeleton frame; it is a steel wall with glazed slots, hypnotically compelling, especially as the eye climbs the rungs of the facade and the glass disappears altogether. Inevitably the black paint makes the effect still more sinister, and the fortress quality is emphasized by the one-story height of the ground floor surmounted by a double height floor accommodating a bank. The only such change in vertical rhythm, this mezzanine level appears to be the true entrance, but, alas, it is no part of the public thoroughfare.

Because the site slopes down to the west, the building sits on a kind of podium of giant steps whose soft, rolled edges make them impossible to use (steel bollards and chains prevent the foolhardy from trying), and real steps are cut into them. The height of the U.S. Steel building was the result of a trade-off with the city, whereby an adjacent narrow block was acquired by the company and turned into a "plaza." The same ground treatment is used here, with the addition of trees regularly distributed. Chiefly because of the hostile steps, the result is a singularly grudging public accommodation all the more remarkable in view of the opportunity that was missed. The desire to repel, even when prompted by the client, would perhaps be more intelligible if there really were some reason why the public should be discouraged from using the plaza or entering the building: here we may again note the phenomenon and delay for a moment a guess as to what it means.

The U.S. Steel building displays the rhetorical possibilities inherent in the design of structure. A quite different statement, but no less rhetorical, is found in Gordon Bunshaft's Marine Midland building nearby at 140 Broadway. Here the architectural statement is not about the nature of structure but of office space. The "function" of the building is recognized as analogous to that of a package; what is offered is a commodity: portions of space. Marine Midland is thus a commodity in a glass and metal wrapping so flat that it appears to have been printed rather than built. If the BMA tower looks like an architectural model, the skin of Marine Midland relates it to recent painting, perhaps the work of Ad Reinhardt, as well as to graphic design in its contrasts of shiny bronze-tinted glass and matte-black metal, seemingly silk-screened over a high-gloss paper. At the same time, its perfect surfaces are contradicted by its actual shape. Marine Midland follows precisely the limits of its site – a block that narrows from east to west, so that the building is a trapezoid four bays wide on the east, three on the west, and seven bays long, the dimensional discrepancy being absorbed in the central core spaces. The reduction of width on the west elevation, although probably unnoticed by thousands of people passing every day, is nevertheless conspicuous when the building is seen from an opposite corner. There is no particular reason why a skyscraper should not follow the contour of an irregular site; what is unnerving here is the distortion of perspective, experienced simultaneously with a prismatically pure, flat mass whose every detail suggests a rigorous formal logic, utterly independent of anything as contingent as a defect in New York's street grid.

Detail is essential to this building, but with one exception it may be said to consist in its own absence: no element on the facade protrudes more than half an inch. The detail that asserts itself as such is a mullion recessed in the center of each column, making the flat surface on either side read as part of the single element incorporating the windows, and yet the extreme delicacy of the mullion (3″ wide) as well as of the glazing bars and the cladding joints, reasserts an underlying affinity with *baukunst*.

The building is surrounded by a field of travertine paving and this, together with a bright red metal cube designed by Isamu Noguchi, completes a tripartite composition. The metal cube, itself out of square and alarmingly balanced on one point, complements the building's distorted perspective. Together the three elements – building, paving, cube – are somehow more than they seem to be, as if the composition had been created by a sculptor of the minimal school intent on transposing the empiricism of architecture into the metaphysics of abstract form. (Are they perfect forms deteriorating toward earthly imperfection, or imperfect forms aspiring to the Platonic Idea?)

That the building follows a now familiar pattern of double height mezzanine with a single height floor at street level, and that its entrances are not generous, seems in this case beside the point. Delicacy of detail tends to overcome an implied indifference to the immediate environment. Marine Midland achieves substantial economies through the design of its flat skin; the formal qualities that derive from this are made explicit through the use of the site. What happens when the flat, two-tone dark skin is applied by the acre to bulk buildings without other distinction is a less happy story. Marine Midland's ubiquitous progeny have not yet matched its distinction, and have introduced a new note to the keyboard of perfunctory solutions to real estate problems; on the other hand they are no more tedious en-masse than the army of vertically pin-striped buildings launched by Mies. In some respects they are more straightforward in recognizing the limits of their own possibilities.

Hancock, U.S. Steel, and Marine Midland have been observed to lack satisfactory relations with the street. In startling contrast is a building that solves this problem, and yet has been criticized because the total form for which its entrance is a necessary solution is unsympathetic to adjacent buildings. The 50-story office tower at 9 West 57th Street in New York City is inserted on an east-west block, where buildings of such height have previously been avoided. Unlike most crosstown streets in Manhattan, 57th is an unusually wide avenue that can absorb 50-story buildings. Since the city exists to make and manage money, it is fatuous to pretend that higher considerations, such as civility, comfort or common sense, can halt the intrusion of these profitable giants; only money can stop what it starts. 9 West 57th Street is controversial, as they say in the newspapers, not because it is tall but because it does not rise straight up from the street (as architects have taught everyone to expect). Ostensibly the result of interpreting the zoning envelope to avoid setbacks, without trading off too much ground area for a "plaza," the building pitches back in a sweeping curve for the first nineteen floors and then rises vertically. This disrupts the continuity of the street and leaves the sides of adjacent buildings exposed; their intersection with the curved glass plane is politely described as unfortunate. However, the bottom of the glass wall is terminated by an enormous trough extending across the full width of the building, carrying off rain water and at the same time providing a generous and explicit entrance canopy. 9 West 57th Street is one of the few skyscrapers recently constructed in New York City of which it can be said that the entrance is neither an inconvenient interruption the architect would rather have avoided, nor an extraneous addition imposed on something else, but is an indispensable part of a unified configuration. Perhaps it is just this contrast, between the agreeable scale at street level and the glass ski-jump looming overhead, that disturbs critics more than the conjunction with buildings on either side. And though critics may agree that it demands a block to itself (imagine it, for example, as a replacement for the UN secretariat) the layman's response is disarmingly contrary to learned opinion. Indeed this building quite literally stops people in the street; the immense curved glass wall is an exhilarating spectacle, not as architecture but as urban theater, as fascinating as a fountain.

The discrepancy between architecture in the service of technique, and architecture in the service of a content for which technique is only the means to an end, generates today's significant arguments about the future of the art. Most of the SOM buildings conceived as expressive form are solutions to non-commercial problems: they are either museums or libraries or schools. Such buildings come into existence because they celebrate something pleasant that has resulted from the accumulation of money, rather than the process by which the money is made. Client and public usually agree that such occasions justify architecture formed, or at least conditioned, by a diet more nourishing than utility. But conventional criticism still finds it necessary to eschew expression (which implies a content to be expressed). If there is such a thing as aristocratic taste (however reluctant it may be to assert itself as such) its distinguishing characteristic in our own time has been its fatigued disavowal of any content other than form itself: there is no message because there is nothing worth saying. Thus "advanced" music denies the emotionally energized expansion and contraction of time, preferring instead the duration of silences between sounds; painting may be nothing more than the sensation of color; architecture only "skin and bones." Arrived finally at its popular level of misunderstanding, the reductionist view achieves ultimate vulgarity in Marshall McLuhan's "the medium is the message": pseudo-technical justification for the vacuous. For Zen priests and Christian mystics perhaps: emptiness and silence are authenticated by the religious disavowal of the self in an indifferent universe, so that emptiness and silence may be filled by ineffable understanding. For us the disavowal of meaning leads more naturally to the empty head.

9 West 57th Street, New York, New York.

How difficult it is, then, to understand buildings that assert a content other than that attributable to their own substance. If the content is intelligible because society has already agreed upon it, the architect may have an easier time. Churches, for example, we do generally agree should look, feel, and be, different from supermarkets, if one feels that churches should exist at all. But monuments? Should they exist? And if so, who is worthy of commemoration? Is a good building honoring an unworthy man all the more reprehensible for accepting the notion of architectural grandeur as psychologically therapeutic and, perhaps, redeeming? The questions are painfully real, despite the infrequent opportunities given to architects to answer them, and criticism seldom rises to the occasion. Thus it is predictable that a monument to an American President, regarded by his enemies as well as his friends as larger than life, should produce critical attacks on the idea of monumentality, rather than on the man himself. The Lyndon Baines Johnson Library in Austin, Texas, matches the idea to the man with a precision all the more disturbing to those who reject the man, yet this building can also be experienced *in vacuo* as the idea of monumentality, a monument in search of a hero, single-minded, undismayed, as unlikely in its time as the appearance of Brahms among the Wagnerites.

Gordon Bunshaft's Johnson Library, true to its circumstances, begins with a tactical display of reticence: placed on a beautiful wooded site, at the end of a major axis on the university campus of which it is a part, the building yields pride of place to a fountain. True, it is a fountain 80 feet in diameter, a white overflowing bowl embedded in a rolling field, but it signifies peaceful intent. The Library itself is off to one side, on a podium approached processionally by a gigantic ramp. Monolithic and calm, the form is immediately intelligible: the building consists of two thick walls tapering as they rise to support a giant roof or attic, itself accommodating the only "work" areas of ritual significance: the President's suite and the study rooms for researchers consulting Presidential papers. Like the massive side walls, the recessed end walls are also of travertine: entrance is below them and under a shelter formed by a balcony. Within, the scale is at first, deliberately and exaggeratedly, pedestrian and disappointing: a 9′ high start toward a room 60′ high and 80′ square, reached by a monumental stair that fills most of the space. At the head of this stair the visitor sees what occasioned the building to begin with: five floors of bookstacks behind a glass wall, holding Presidential papers in thousands of red leather boxes ornamented by gold Presidential seals. Subordinate, low-ceilinged exhibition areas open off one end of this hall, as they surround the monumental stair that starts on the floor below. At each end of the main floor (a rectangle exactly twice as long as it is wide) the visitor can step out onto a balcony, from which the views are variously of the landscaped Library grounds, the long, low, adjacent building housing schools of political sciences, the campus, a stadium, and motels. Small town detritus is not enough to break a mood: this place is different from other places; people have come here because, in addition to wanting amusement, there is something important in the air. Understanding, acceptance, or rejection is sustained: scale and form signify the extraordinary, and most people find beautiful whatever removes them from their own lives. The critic may observe that the end walls, being thin and flat and plainly screens, might well have been of another material; the travertine-clad framing of the glass bookstack wall may be superfluous; and the thick, tapering side walls have no relation to the conventional column structure they conceal. But these are critics' details, and no detail outweighs the genuine achievement: this is a monument equal to a man Americans will remember for a long time. It is architecture in the service of emotion, and like many buildings whose significance is their capacity for inducing exaltation, this one serves in ways that were not foreseen. It has become a place to visit even when it is closed to the public. At night, when there is little to do in Austin, the podium is dotted with couples in quiet conversation, bicycles resting against the parapet, heads turning occasionally to contemplate the massive curved walls, shadowed and unrevealing, as problematic as the man who caused them to be built.

In the Johnson Library Bunshaft is content to write his own exegesis on the load bearing wall of antiquity, concluding that its role as sculptural mass needs no explicit structural justification. His Beinecke Library for rare books, at Yale University, doubtless because it protects intrinsically valuable works of the printer's art rather than the records of a government, uses structure and materials to suggest value, care, and expense. Like a crystal casket inside a marble box, the book storage case of this library is a glass-enclosed air-conditioned building in itself. Surrounded by an ambulatory and bathed in the warm light cast by walls of translucent Vermont marble, the interior makes it clear that something

Lyndon Baines Johnson Library, University of Texas, Austin, Texas.

worth preserving is here enshrined. The outer marble walls, held in a structural lattice so articulated that it scarcely appears to function as a flat truss, are lifted above ground by four squat, tapered concrete columns. Small size is proper to the rare and precious, and this has been achieved by removing from the program of functions to be made manifest almost all of the strictly utilitarian office and work spaces; only a sunk plaza open to the sky reveals their underground existence. Like a Fabergé Easter egg the building titillates by being seriously frivolous, but unlike courtly amusements it is made respectable by its association with learning. Yet its architect has himself been hesitant: the closer one approaches to the books the more the language of form reverts to ordinary structuralism. At the heart of the shrine one finds the detail of a refined office building; the discrepancy is scarcely fatal, but suggests the difficulty we now have in coping with architectural events that require the superfluous embellishment, rather than the utilitarian essential. Notwithstanding, the Beinecke Library delights, as it was meant to do.

The expressive themes of Bunshaft's buildings recall classical architecture, and the means he finds most suitable for their realization are the podium and the attic. Both are used directly in the Johnson Library; the Beinecke Library transforms them, so that the ground plane is revealed to be a podium only by the hole cut into it, while the roof is implied by walls which, rooflike, are lifted above the ground. Quotations from the classics, however, are not alone responsible for the vaguely Beaux Arts aura of these and other SOM buildings. It is perhaps due more to the willingness – indeed the determination – to contain intricate and highly differentiated facilities in a shell that denies or obscures their presence, and to organize these spaces around circulation systems which, because they are big but seldom grand, are often inert.

It is not an oversight in presentation that the plans of SOM's buildings, considered as graphic compositions in themselves, are their least interesting aspect. Intention, like interest, is most sharply focused on a three-dimensional form to which the plan is subordinate, but the form often lacks the animation that can come from a plan interesting in itself. That this should be so is perhaps unremarkable for offices and other commercial buildings; but it is a conspicuous difference between SOM's work (with the exception of Walter Netsch) and that of other comparable architects. Some of the problems involved in this are fundamental to the structuralist point of view; others are a matter of temperament and, therefore, of procedure. So, for example, a particular structural system is selected either because there is no other way to achieve the desired result, or because it evokes a certain character regardless of its side effects. In either case a decision regarding scale is accepted a priori; planning proceeds from it as the fitting into a container of spaces that may or may not require their own local adjustments. Thus the Johnson Library suggests on its exterior that it accommodates a gigantic room. This is in fact the case, but only for one half of the building; the other half, accommodating storage and work areas mostly inaccessible to the public and inimical to the architect's intention, is equally absorbed in the same monumental mass.

Beinecke Rare Book and Manuscript Library, Yale University, New Haven, Connecticut.

The kind of forced fit associated with bulk planning is conventionally more acceptable, if not more satisfying, when its justification is structural efficiency and logic. But when the formal determinant is an expressive intention other than that implied by structure, current sensibility tends to resist what is, after all, an assertion made by the architect about the meaning and value of his work. The nature of the profession being what it is, architects who are unable or unwilling to make such assertions are unlikely to survive as architects. Private shop talk among professionals, like folk wisdom, often recognizes the psychological factors involved; public discussion, at least as it has been largely influenced by the querulous style of English journalism, conveniently ignores the objective realities that sustain psychological patterns, preferring instead to attribute an unhappy outcome solely to the architects' natural perversity. Objective reality includes, besides everything else normally indicated by the term, the history of architecture and the history of a particular architect. It is by now a celebrated fact that modern architecture cannot cope with history – even its own. Thus shop talk grudgingly acknowledges selected pages in the various monographs of Le Corbusier or Mies, but public criticism rarely refers to the controlling influence of such specific methods and attitudes inherited from the recent past. The four methods of composition outlined by Le Corbusier in the first volume of Boesiger's monograph, for example, are still the armature on which architects hang their ideas (even though two of those methods have been found less useful in practice) and their use has distinct, predictable consequences. So, for example, the first diagram proposes the articulation of functions or spaces in shapes that can both compete and contrast with each other. Such contrasts lead to discontinuity: different treatments of facades on the same volume, or the breaking up of a volume into components ever more qualified (but still determined by some aspect of space or function, not structure). Because such qualifications tend to be costly, they are apt to be limited to small buildings and perhaps most suitably to houses. The specific advantages of the method are the increased range in scale; the heightening of interest where that is appropriate; and the possibility of a genuine response to a functional problem. The disadvantages are the competitive restlessness generated by discontinuity, especially in the urban context; and the difficulty of finding spaces or functions that can reasonably be given separate identity. Yet the alternative to an architecture determined by Miesian structural regularity has so far been keyed to this mode, whether it employs the suave curves and surfaces of early Le Corbusier or the harder shapes and materials associated with Brutalism. The expressive range the method makes possible leads to its being criticized for just the virtues said to be lacking in the structuralist approach, which is thought to offend for its repetitiveness, its often inflexible scale, and its unresponsiveness to functional distinctions.

The other well-known alternative available to architects is a plan module so finely grained that it allows – indeed demands – maximum maneuverability. Wright used a 2′ × 4′ rectangle for this purpose, and achieved even greater flexibility with the hexagon. The advantage of the method (and even Wright had method) is that it encourages variety within continuity. Wright had other ways to achieve that, of course, including his occasional experiments with the 45 degree angle in plan (made feasible for his colleagues by Louis Kahn, and by James Stirling who has developed it with still greater flexibility of shape, section, and surface). It is therefore curious that the plan as such has received so little attention in recent polemics, and doubly curious that in the United States it should be an SOM partner, Walter Netsch, who has made this problem central to his work.

The term "field theory" as used by Netsch to describe his method (he would prefer to say, process) is problematic for architectural discourse in that it derives from other disciplines. Of the meanings collected around it, those associated with behavioral science are perhaps uppermost in his mind: in this context what is referred to is a method of analyzing events as the interplay of diverse "sociocultural, biomechanical, and motivational forces." Putting aside the unappetizing tautologies of behaviorism, it may also be recalled that in physics a field is "a space in which magnetic or electric lines of force are active," and more generally "the area or space under the influence of, or within the range of, some agent." These latter definitions suggest that a field is a passive subject; the former that it is an active agent. Both aspects are appropriate to its architectural employment, and to them should be added the concern of Gestalt psychology: the organically perceptual whole whose configuration cannot be reduced to, or built up from, simple "atomic" elements of sensation. In this context "field" qualities belong to the whole but not to its parts, and in an architectural plan derived from particles or modules of space the product should be a whole perceptually different from its components. What Netsch has developed is a set of components that may or may not be intended by him to meet the requirements of a Gestalt percept; he does intend them to reveal, and to generate, architectural possibilities more numerous and more satisfying than those otherwise available.

The specifics of the method are simple enough: squares of identical or varying size are overlaid and rotated. The resultant diagonals produce an interlocking second grid of octagons; to which a third or a fourth may be added when their scale and placement yield further useful subdivisions. Graphically these patterns resemble, and are direct descendants of, the complicated wall decorations of Arabian architecture and the optically disturbing window lattices of 17th century Muslim architecture in India, notably at the tomb of I'timad-ud-Daulah at Agra, and at Fatehpur-Sikri. These lattices employ interlocking patterns that are multi-axial, but because they give equal stress to two or more axes, comprehension of their pattern structure requires the observer to select one axis around which to organize the components of the others as "subordinate." Since the designers of these patterns might craftily choose to place them askew within an orthogonal architectural setting (a window frame, for instance) the observer's choice of a single axis to "read" as dominant requires an act of will, sometimes contrary to information supplied by the immediate architectural environment. The result is a kind of optical shock, a physiological derangement incomparably more subtle than any of its recent counterparts in Western op art. To press such patterns into the service of architectural planning may perhaps seem gratuitous, but there is no inherent reason why the abstract decorative arts of Asia should be less instructive to Western architects than, say, the orthogonal compositions of Mondrian and van Doesburg. Neither is it any the less plausible to rationalize the use of a plan module rather than a structural system. The only pertinent test of their value, presumably, is whether or not they make better buildings.

What is a better building? In Netsch's view it is one that contains, implicit in its plan, simultaneously coexisting possibilities for movement and development. A dense lattice contains too many possibilities: the plan is finally what survives after the architect has erased those possibilities he does not need; but their existence as an after-image is always sustained by what remains. Thus in theory the recent buildings Netsch has designed for the Chicago campus of the University of Illinois (Architecture and Art; Behavioral Sciences; Science and Engineering) might be said to contain not only themselves but also each other. In practice the observer, like the architect, is confronted with some serious problems. Foremost among them is the problem of intelligibility. These buildings require many small interior spaces, and their relation to each other must be signalled by some constant factor. On the two-dimensional paper plan all is clear because all is simultaneous; in the three-dimensional reality all is unclear because, alas, the observer can be in only one place at a time. Here in fact is one generalization that can be drawn from the angles, turns, and corners generated by Netsch's geometry: like the English "picturesque" their appeal is in their irregularity; but unlike the picturesque they require not a fixed, preferred standpoint from which the whole is best seen, but rather an extended tour with a map in hand.

Where this problem refers to the interiors it may be partly resolved by a spatial element that can be perceived in its entirety; the obvious candidate is the circulation system. But it is precisely here that Netsch chooses to break corridors into short lengths with frequent turns, occasionally amplifying them into programmed multiple-use spaces too similar to serve as landmarks and too distracting to maintain the sense of direction. A stabilizing frame comparable to that found in Muslim pattern design is omitted, and the result is disorientation as a normative condition. But externally the results are more gratifying, firstly because the faceted elevations produced by the plan-pattern are accessible in amounts sufficient to suggest the underlying principle of organization; and secondly because the program of a given building usually contains some element substantially different in scale and character, thereby providing the necessary stabilizing contrast.

The cardinal advantage of a multi-axial plan geometry is its capacity to respond to exceptional situations – to qualify and particularize what might by other means be merely accommodated or obscured, or suppressed. Such amplification is humanly sympathetic: it relishes difference and seeks to enhance it. But to do so it must also depend on the availability of real occasions for complexity: what is inimical to its purpose is a situation that is genuinely simple. Where the plan deals with a multi-story building it tends to reject complexity for the vertical section, but where the architect is dealing with a one- or two-story building, particularly on an irregular site, and where it is possible to

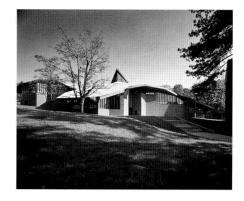

Louis Jefferson Long Library, Wells College, Aurora, New York.

Carlton Centre, Johannesburg, South Africa.

University of Illinois, Chicago Circle Campus, Chicago, Illinois.

Macy's Rego Park, Queens, New York.

utilize the roof as a visibly articulated element, expressive possibilities are increased. Interesting examples are the pavilions of the Winnebago Children's Home in Neillsville and the Louis Jefferson Long Library at Wells College, in Aurora, New York. The library's plan is organized by nine interlocking clusters of rotated, overlapping squares, together with two or perhaps three different kinds of residual spaces between them. Because the squares are shifted within the lattice (to allow for the varying residual spaces) the basic pin-wheel plan is difficult to grasp except in diagram form. Prow-like projections and a rambling, pitched, timber roof produce five elevations which can be read as concavities – recessions that seem to invite rather than repel entrance. Awkward as some of the forms may be, the result is a building that deserves comparison with related work by Aalto and, more importantly, by Frank Lloyd Wright; the latter would have been hard put to deny the presence here of what he urged architects to seek: the "principle" with which they could generate their own effects.

Among the problems Netsch's "field theory" might be expected to solve, with greater success than has heretofore been seen, is that of relating buildings to each other on extended sites. On the Chicago Campus of the University of Illinois, where Netsch is dealing with isolated and by-passing rectangular blocks in an earlier neo-plastic layout of his own devising, the problem is largely untouched because the buildings are so dispersed. The textural continuity implied by his three most recent buildings remains unrealized. Here we touch on a problem endemic to modern architecture, and one that requires an extended discussion not entirely germane to all of the buildings under review. Yet some generalizations are in order: all of them have to do with the pernicious influence of the garden city idea, and Le Corbusier's version of it in particular. By now we should need no further proof that the preoccupation with the integrity of built form renders architectural civility impossible. Buildings can be laws unto themselves, but only at the expense of the architectural community. No juxtaposition of large-scale buildings in the urban context, however skillfully they may be displayed like objects on a table, can compensate for their fundamental lack of necessary conjunction. Yet the formal integrity of the free-standing building remains the touchstone of site planning, and the greater the architect's success, the more problematic is the effect on the fabric of our cities. Thus Carlton Centre, in Johannesburg, South Africa, is no doubt as skillful a juxtaposition as may be expected of towers whose bulk is determined by non-architectural considerations, and the public space the composition yields is more coherent than most – but it is also possible to imagine similar results with an entirely different and equally arbitrary composition.

SOM's memorable achievements in site planning have been at one or another end of the scale of possibilities: either an exceptionally difficult situation involving the shape and location of a single building; or a situation of seemingly unlimited happy possibilities. In the first category may be considered two quite different buildings: the Hirshhorn Museum, on the Mall in Washington, D.C., and adjacent to the Smithsonian Institution; and the department store for Macy's in Queens, New York. In the latter case a triangular site, in the former the necessity for inserting a form of minimal resistance to its environment, yield circular buildings as the ideal solution, and in both cases the form is conspicuously successful. When scale is modest, planning problems of the second category sometimes seem to resolve themselves with form that aspires to the qualities of folk architecture, inserting buildings into the landscape with tact and reticence. Thus the Carmel Valley Manor housing in California, a residential complex for retired people comprising numerous small buildings, each with several apartments, together with related community facilities, offers a regional echo of the Spanish colonial vernacular. Beguiling in photographs, the actual effect is both more subtle and more substantial. Amenities of the site are enhanced; open but sheltered courts connect and stabilize what might have been too dispersed; patently decorative arches add continuity; and pitched roofs provide agreeable variety and interest. Indeed the entire composition achieves the kind of relaxed "ordinariness" advocated during the last several years by Robert Venturi and others, and it also employs design elements with attractive associations for the people who use the buildings – but it does this without the patronizing sarcasm that tends to make such exercises a kind of "in" joke among architects, as distinguished from the adult effort to please. The architectural smirk – its proponents prefer to call it a taste for irony – has been much admired lately; perhaps that is why this straightforward project, like the short-lived Bay Region style before it, has been so little noticed; it achieved effortlessly what now seems to require the heaving and straining of "theory."

Carmel Valley Manor, Carmel Valley, California.

Poise and spontaneity may be possible only in rural circumstances; the San Francisco office's attempt to accommodate to a difficult urban situation, by mediating between the demands of the street and the demands of architecture, has produced one interesting but dubious exercise in scenic design. The problem was to add a hotel tower to San Francisco's Union Square, but without disrupting the relatively uniform height of existing facades. The solution was to set the tower well back from the street, interposing a lower wing (for public rooms) conforming with adjacent buildings as it faces Union Square, but cut back from the side street at a forty-five degree angle to produce, and at the same time conceal, an entrance plaza that avoids competing with the Square itself. The result is a facade like a Hollywood stage flat; when seen from the corner it appears to have no building behind it, an effect that naturally rivets attention on itself. The arched window openings, however they were intended, are out of scale, and a disembodied facade is a somewhat cavalier gesture toward urban politesse; yet the result is not entirely unpersuasive, and one ends by wanting it to work.

An interesting counterpart to this kind of urban theater is the Mauna Kea Beach Hotel on the island of Hawaii. Merely to name the building is to state the problem, conjuring up visions of tropical fantasies, yet what distinguishes the building is that, while it is indeed architecture-at-play, it remains rational architecture of a high order. Four stories on the beach side, three inland, with a detached dining pavilion, the hotel's architectural character derives from the inward stagger of its three guest floors above a series of central courts open to the sky. Sheltered open-air corridors thus overlook thoroughly landscaped gardens, and it is these corridors and bridges that lend an air of Piranesian complexity. Individual rooms, each with a balcony, are furnished lightly and almost casually; elsewhere the sense of "decor" is sustained by furnishings and decorations chosen from several countries, and constituting a highly sophisticated appraisal of "good design" as that term might be understood (and rejected) by a knowledgeable professional.

By popular agreement the climate and history of San Francisco can be held responsible for more relaxed attitudes, but whatever the reason it does seem to be the case that SOM's West Coast offices are less preoccupied with the formal justification of their work. Essays in structural calisthenics (Alcoa) are rare: the structural imperative does not have the same self-justifying persuasiveness in San Francisco that it has in Chicago. Nor is San Francisco particularly interested in forcing from high-rise structure its most operatic interludes: The Bank of America building, Egyptian in its polished, marbled grandeur, is after all an essay in the use of bay windows (curiously anticipating some aspects of the Sears Tower massing). Yet SOM's best work in the engineer's idiom is to be found nearby in Oakland: Edward Bassett's Oakland-Alameda Coliseum, based on earlier studies by Myron Goldsmith for a similar problem, is a genuinely convincing match of "pure" structural form to the actual situation and program. The arena and stadium are structures of comparable mass: their siting in relation to the highway, and the use of earth berms to reduce apparent bulk, are skillful and unaggressive; the circular concave roof suspended above an oval arena yields an intensely dynamic space, without embellishment, and difficult problems of plan and structure are resolved with unforced elegance.

In this context of low-keyed engineering on the one hand, and almost casual experiment on the other, it is perhaps surprising that the San Francisco office should have produced one of the most important of SOM's recent buildings: Edward Bassett's office for the Weyerhaeuser Company, on a rural site near Tacoma, Washington. The exurban office building, like the Beaux Arts "Palace for a Head of State," constitutes the modern "ideal" problem. Because such corporate headquarters are intended to attract employees by offering the most congenial environment, and because they stand serene in private parks, they avoid the overbearing, competitive, and increasingly ominous tone of their urban counterparts. When supplemented by collections of modern art, as is often the case, these buildings and their sites become local attractions sought out by the public. That some employees nevertheless feel trapped in paradise raises another kind of question, best left to Sunday supplement psychologists, but the fact remains that exurban corporate headquarters are architectural improvements of the environment as a result of decentralization.

The principal architectural distinction of the Weyerhaeuser building is that it is conceived as part of its site, in that metaphorical sense characteristic of Frank Lloyd Wright. This is not to say that it relies on Wrightian geometry and texture to make it seem literally an extension of the ground; but rather that its component parts are dominated by the idea of a building as an abstraction of the site's contours. Inevitably the result is formal emphasis on horizontal lines and masses, with vertical structure subordinate. At Weyerhaeuser

Bank of America Headquarters, San Francisco, California.

Oakland-Alameda County Coliseum, Oakland, California.

Headquarters of the Weyerhaeuser Company, Tacoma, Washington.

Mauna Kea Beach Hotel, Kamuela, Hawaii.

parapets and columns alike are given minimal detailing. In this respect it makes a striking contrast with SOM's other major work in the genre, Gordon Bunshaft's office complex for the American Can Company, in Greenwich, Connecticut. Like Weyerhaeuser, American Can is set as a wall across its site, in the process creating an artificial lake. But where the Weyerhaeuser building is consistently and exclusively conceived as a pyramidal stack of trays or terraces, American Can presents itself as a three-story pavilion on a massive podium. The Weyerhaeuser solution is dependent on outdoor accommodations for cars; American Can's podium accommodates five floors of concealed parking. There are other major differences: at American Can executive offices are housed in a completely separate pavilion; comparable Weyerhaeuser accommodations are handled as an integral penthouse. The American Can pavilions open on interior courts. The Weyerhaeuser building, using the deep floors made possible by "office landscape" planning, is oriented entirely outward to the view. In both buildings refinements of structure serve important purposes. For American Can precast concrete double-web beams in constructivist detail produce elevations alternately over-scaled or delicate. At Weyerhaeuser round columns are arranged in a diagrid, which has the critical advantage of making successive setbacks at each floor read quite clearly, regardless of light or detail, because the unaligned columns introduce depth perspective.

Both buildings are preeminently rational solutions. Weyerhaeuser avoids all classicizing references and attempts to engage itself directly with its site, yet it may be argued that terraced car parks are not an improvement to the landscape. As with all horizontally articulated buildings, there are problems about how and where to end, and for that matter the copper-clad hipped roof of the penthouse level is a peculiarly domestic conclusion. Some of these problems are avoided at American Can by virtue of its self-containing podium, which not only leaves the landscape free of automobiles but allows an agreeably theatrical flourish: an access road that peels off into multilevel ramps vanishing into the podium. More accomplished in its handling of interior space, as well as in landscape details, the American Can complex elicits admiration but perhaps not the excitement of Weyerhaeuser's underlying idea, however incompletely realized it may be. At Weyerhaeuser some dimly remembered lesson of Wright's seems to offer an Ariadne's thread out of the intellectual labyrinth of perfect structure. Both buildings are major achievements.

The critic's conventional excuse for refraining from definitive appraisals of current work – apart from the fear of becoming a comic footnote on the pages of history – is that we are too close in time to sort out the real significance of what seems at first very good, very bad, or merely indifferent. But of course such judgments are made from moment to moment, by architects even more than critics, and the critic who advises architects to take more risks ought to be willing to take some himself. Which of the buildings reviewed here will survive? In ten years which ones will seem worth visiting; which ones will have to be included in histories of American building, either because they established a new possibility or because they seemed in their perfection to close a line of development once and for all?

Joseph H. Hirshhorn Museum and Sculpture Garden, Washington, D.C.

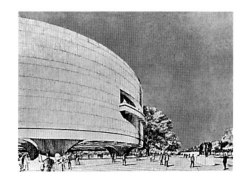

Wright observed that every great thing is too much of whatever it is. If that is true, it must also apply to such problematic ventures as the Hancock tower or 9 West 57th Street: both are too much of what they are, and yet both are likely to survive in the popular imagination, growing in sentimental associations like the Eiffel Tower, which they resemble.

The Johnson and Beinecke libraries, qualitatively different, are also likely to grow in esteem because they offer experiences most architects are unwilling to grant. That the Johnson Library achieves monumentality through mass, with its concomitant historical associations, in no way invalidates the desire for monumentality. There is a kind of malnutrition, or vitamin deficiency, attributable to the modern utilitarian style: we are perishing of undernourishment but cannot bring ourselves to recognize the ailment. Those architects who do, and who try to offer a more balanced diet, find themselves accused of offering cake while the populace lacks bread. The Beinecke Library is one of those rare essays in architectural pleasure, for the public, and it has been so accepted and appreciated.

At the other end of the spectrum are those buildings really meant for architects: the BMA tower, for instance, must surely be the perfect, and the last, statement on the theme. Marine Midland, and the numerous other buildings SOM has executed in its flat style, may be as close as we can get to folk architecture (or good bread). Less dependent than is Mies' system of structural articulation on the refinement of an individual's sensibility, the style lends itself to easy adaptation. The Sears Tower would seem likely to break the spell of single-volume tower design, suggesting a flexibility more appropriate to the actual problems, even if the Sears Tower itself does not solve them all. This willingness to experiment with the plan, even more than with the structure, is carried furthest in Walter Netsch's "field theory" buildings for the University of Illinois. Though each of them seems only partly successful, the attempt to provide a rational basis for complex plan geometry is a real alternative to the chic but pointless abuses of nonrectilinear planning. It is much to SOM's credit that "research" includes the examination of ideas, as well as technique.

The American Can and Weyerhaeuser buildings must surely be counted as likely candidates for long life, the one because it is beautiful, the other because it seems to reveal the underlying compatibility between Wright's sense of architecture as landscaping and Mies' early clarification of Wright without benefit of romantic rhetoric. Weyerhaeuser is in some respects a Miesian diagram of certain Wright projects of the 1920's, and it may well help to focus attention on promising possibilities.

The character of architecture is determined by the kinds of problems architects are asked to solve. Like most other architects, SOM has not yet persuaded its clients that their problems are sometimes improperly defined. Among such problems those created by the urban high-rise building are foremost. As the detailing and structure of the skyscraper become more sophisticated, the buildings themselves become more disturbing. It is as if we were striving to design a really beautiful electric chair: the fault is not in the style but in the thing itself.

In the 1950's immense effort was expended to convince clients and zoning boards that skyscrapers should be set back from the building line, if that was the price to be paid for a vertical rise without setbacks. If it was possible to induce that behavior, it is scarcely surprising that the well-established offices should now be expected to educate their clients to somewhat more desirable notions of civic responsibility. Architects will be able to persuade their clients that the street, for example, is part of the building – but only after they have persuaded themselves.

Perhaps the most urgent task confronting the architect is to ameliorate the conflict between private indifference and public well-being: in that respect the battle for modern architecture is a long way from being won. SOM's contribution has been not merely technical brilliance and a standard of professionalism second to none; it has been a champion for desirable change. Having written some of the best passages of American architectural history, it now seems fair that SOM should be expected to perform as well in the next phase.

Headquarters of the American Can Company, Greenwich, Connecticut.

Skidmore, Owings & Merrill

Partners 1973

Gordon Bunshaft

J. Walter Severinghaus

William E. Hartmann

Walter A. Netsch

John O. Merrill, Jr.

David H. Hughes

Roy O. Allen

Edward C. Bassett

Bruce J. Graham

David A. Pugh

Myron Goldsmith

Albert Lockett

Walter H. Costa

Donald C. Smith

Marc E. Goldsmith

Fazlur R. Khan

Whitson M. Overcash

James R. DeStefano

Robert Diamant

Thomas J. Eyerman

Richard E. Lenke

Michael A. McCarthy

Leon Moed

John K. Turley

Gordon L. Wildermuth

Consulting Partner

Nathaniel A. Owings

Macy's Rego Park, Queens, New York

The building has an excellent location relating to the intersection of Queens Boulevard passing to the south and the Long Island Expressway to the east, which are the two major traffic arteries serving this area.

Sales areas and parking facilities are combined in a single cylindrical building, 426' in diameter, which occupies the southern portion of an irregular site. The elegant perforated facade is formed by poured-in-place concrete which has been sandblasted to expose a coarse white aggregate. The perforations permit the natural ventilation of the garage levels which surround the inner core sales floors.

Parking is provided for 1,250 cars on five ring levels above the plaza and on the roof of the top sales floor. The arrangement provides the customer with the convenience of "curb-side parking" or a very short walk to the sales areas. Two double-helical ramps provide computer-controlled access to the parking levels. The core of the helices contains mechanical equipment areas.

There are three sales floors containing a total area of approximately 270,000 sq ft. The largest sales floor is on the ground level and extends beneath the first garage level 30'. The remaining area forms a shopper's arcade with display windows and adjoins a landscaped plaza. A basement level is provided for storage and contains trucking service facilities with access from a ramp beneath the helices.

The building has been designed to expand one sales floor and two parking levels.

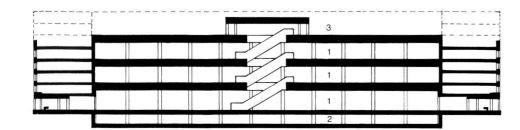

Section of the building.
1 Sales area
2 Deliveries
3 Parking facilities
The broken line indicates a possible future addition.

Entrance and exit ramps to and from the ▷
parking levels.   24

View of the department store from across
Queens Boulevard.

Plans (ground floor, typical floor).
1 Queens Boulevard
2 55th Avenue
3 Justice Avenue
4 56th Avenue
5 Sales area
6 Arcade
7 Entrance ramp
8 Exit ramp
9 Down and up ramps to and from service
  basement
10 Garage ring

Close-up of the building. ▷

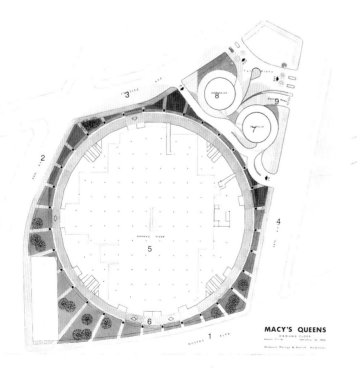

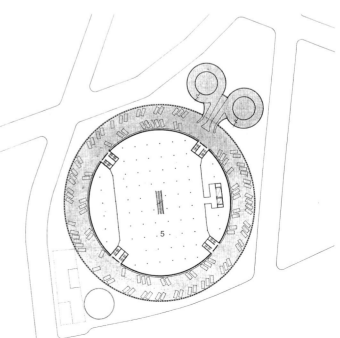

MACY'S QUEENS

Publishing House and Printing Plant of the Newspaper "The Republic," Columbus, Indiana

The new building for the newspaper, which celebrated its centenary in 1972, is situated in the center of the town, directly opposite the historic Bartholomew County Courthouse. It represents an important part of the redevelopment plan for the town center, also prepared by Skidmore, Owings & Merrill, which provides among other facilities for an enclosed shopping mall extending over two blocks.

The ground floor covers an area of 256′ × 96′. On the west side are a cafeteria, the staff offices, the management offices as well as the accounting department. To the east of these is a lobby which extends across the building from one long side to the other. Adjacent to the south side of the lobby is the editorial department, on the north side the advertising department. Also on the north side are the composing and printing plants. At the eastern end of the ground floor is the delivery zone. In the basement below the printing plant and delivery zone, covering an area of 96′ × 96′, are the paper store, the paper feed to the printing machine as well as mechanical installations. The paper rolls are delivered by means of an elevator outside the building which, when not in use, is covered by a slab flush with the ground.

While the internal columns in the ground floor are on a grid of 32′ × 32′, those along the facades are spaced at 10′8″ so as to permit an integration of facade and bearing structure and thereby to convey an impression of extreme lightness. An independent foundation below the printing machine ensures that machine vibrations are not transferred to the building. Measures have also been taken to prevent noise disturbance from the printing process. The noise level of 90 decibels experienced in the printing section is reduced by special glass walls so that, in the other rooms, no more than a slight humming noise can be heard which does not rise beyond the general noise level.

To expose the newspaper operation as much as possible to the outside, the building is almost wholly glazed.

Plan.
1 Lobby
2 Cafeteria
3 Staff office
4 Management offices
5 Accounting department
6 Editor's office
7 Advertising department
8 Composing plant
9 Printing plant
10 Deliveries
11 Elevator to basement

Cafeteria. On the rear wall, the sign of the ▷ company, which used to be mounted on the old building of the newspaper.

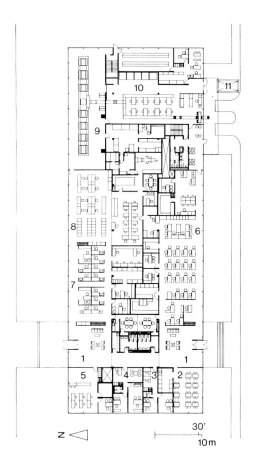

Bartholomew County Courthouse, seen from the printing plant. West side of the building.

◁ West side of the building. Here are cafeteria, staff office, management office and accounting.

North side of the building. In the foreground, the printing plant. Through the large glass walls, the newspaper-making process is fully exposed to the passer-by.

Philip Morris Cigarette Manufacturing Plant, Richmond, Virginia. Under construction

The site on which the factory is being erected covers an area of 125 acres. A large oval reflecting pool and extensive landscaping with formally and informally arranged groups of trees will help to give the site a park-like character.

The plant itself has a total area of 1,700,000 sq ft. All buildings are of steel frame construction clad with precast concrete panels.

The cigarette making and packing plant proper, covering an area of 212′ × 1,000′, must be regarded as one of the largest of its kind in the world. The first floor is divided into five compartments and is spanned by trusses 23′ high without intermediate columns. This entire area is exclusively reserved for cigarette making and packing; ancillary spaces not directly concerned with the manufacturing process – air conditioning plant, toilets, lounges, etc. – are accommodated in tower-like structures 96′ high, which provide vertical accents to the otherwise predominantly horizontal mass. These towers serve not only the main building but also two parallel buildings, one for the administration, the other for workshops and the manufacture of filters. The spaces between the main building and these ancillary buildings are landscaped luxuriant gardens.

On the south side of this central core area is a large, square building for the primary processing of the tobacco. Another building on the west side serves as a warehouse, with unloading and loading facilities for supplies and finished goods.

All buildings except the warehouse are fully air-conditioned.

Site plan. ▷
1 Tobacco processing
2 Cigarette making and packing
3 Filter manufacture
4 Workshops
5 Supply warehouse
6 Finished goods warehouse
7 Administration
8 Power plant

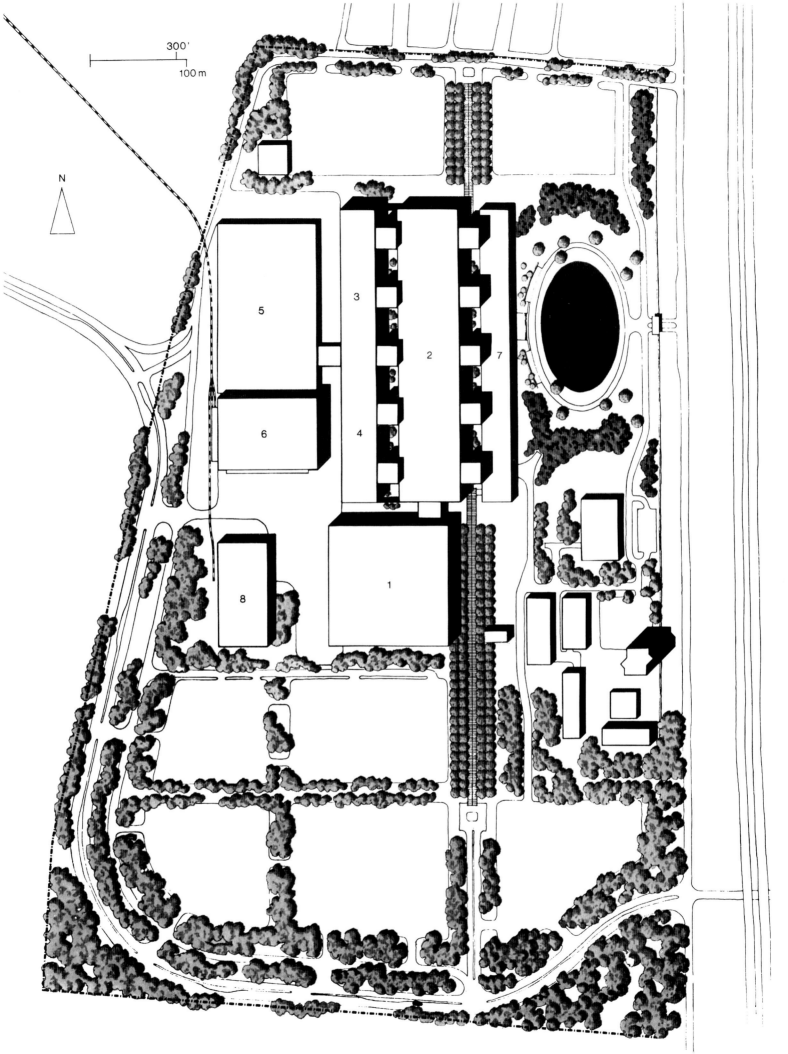

View from northeast (model).

Cross-section through the central complex. On the left, the administration building; in the center, the cigarette making and packing plant; on the right, the workshops and filter manufacturing room.

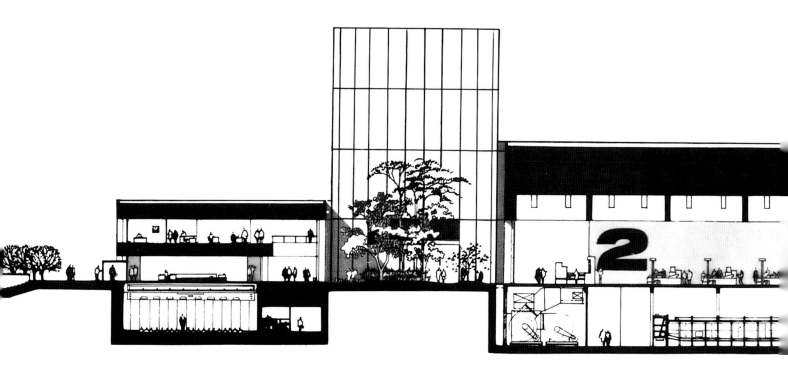

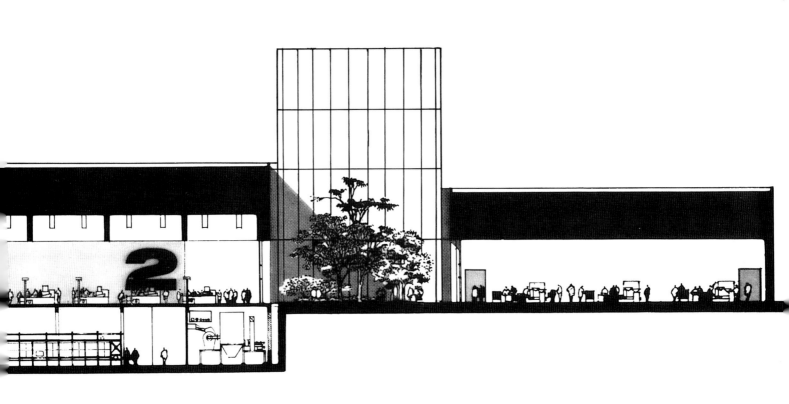

Central Engineering Building of the Armstrong Cork Company, Lancaster, Pennsylvania

The building, accommodating some 200 staff members of the development section of the internationally known manufacturer of building materials, is situated at the edge of the company's land surrounded by a large lawn.

The upper level is a column-free space about 11'6" high with a narrow core and a few floor-to-ceiling glass partitions. In addition to some conference rooms and offices and a small reference library of technical books, this floor accommodates four large drafting rooms for engineers and architects. The ground floor, only about 9' high and divided by columns, contains entrance lobby, administrative offices, cafeteria, archives and a drafting room for designers. On the basement level are service rooms and display rooms for the company's products.

The externally exposed, black painted steel framework clearly reveals the structural system. At the roof, for instance, a clear distinction is made between the short sides where the main girders, spanning about 117', emerge into the open, and the long sides with their secondary beams above the non-bearing cladding. A view of the short sides also provides an instant appreciation of the closer column spacing at ground floor level which permitted to size the intermediate ceiling about three times less deep than the roof. The structural system is also clearly emphasized by the deep setback (about 8') of the floor-to-ceiling glass walls and by the white painted undersides of suspended ceiling and roof.

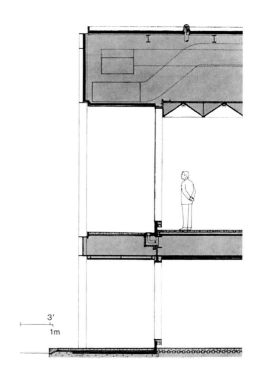

3'
1m

Facade section. The roof, which spans the entire width of the building, is about three times as high as the intermediate ceiling which is supported by columns on a grid of 16'8" × 29'2".

Corner of the building. The black painted steel ▷ structure is clearly distinguishable from the recessed glass walls.

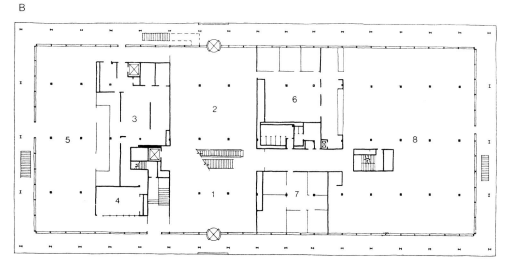

One of the short sides of the building. The intermediate columns at the ground floor show clearly in this view.

Plans.
A Ground floor
B Upper floor
1 Entrance lobby
2 Central cloakroom
3 Kitchen
4 Dining room
5 Cafeteria
6 Reference library
7 Offices and conference rooms
8 Designers
9 Project engineers
10 Specialities engineers
11 Architects and engineers

Part of the long facade. The steel framework ▷
is externally exposed and painted black.

38

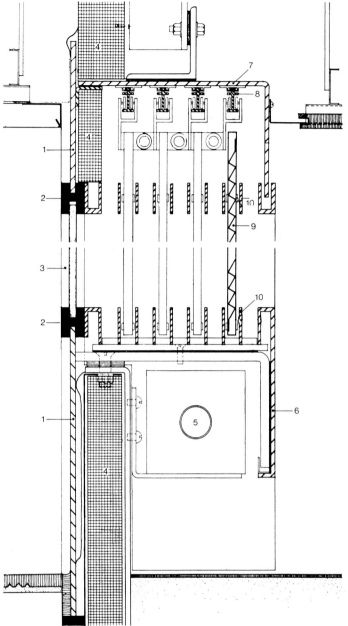

Apart from the deep setback of the glass,
sun protection is also provided by internally
mounted steel sunshades, 25″ wide, which run
on plastic rails above the radiators.

Detail of outer wall.
 1 Steel plate
 2 Plastic frame
 3 Glass
 4 Rigid insulation
 5 Radiator
 6 Radiator cover
 7 Holding rail for metal sunshades
 8 Track
 9 Metal sunshade
10 Guide rail

The prismatic panels of the upper floor ceiling, each carrying two unconcealed fluorescent lamps, emphasize the basic building module of 50″ × 50″. Fresh air enters through perforations in the panels, return air escapes through slots adjacent to the light fixtures. The space is divided by module-wide glass partitions, held at top and bottom only. Compared with a level ceiling, the prismatic panels have the advantage of providing a better dispersal of the light, a more effective sound absorption, and a more accentuated faceting of the space.

Headquarters of the Boots Pure Drug Company, Nottingham, England

This building, in which about 1,300 people work, is situated on a former storage site in an industrial estate 10 minutes by car from the town center. The move had been decided despite the fact that, in recent years, a number of new buildings had been erected at the old location in the town center.

Because of the large site it was possible, in designing the building, to assign a predominant role to such considerations as economical construction methods and efficient organization of work. The result was a low-rise, two-story building with an interior court, covering an area of 480' × 288'. About one-half of the lower floor is below natural ground level and another quarter is concealed behind a sloped in-filling of excavated soil so that the upper floor is the only one visible. Its structural steel frame consists of cruciform columns and of truss girders bridging bays of 96' side length. Surrounding the interior court at upper floor level is a continuous open-plan office area. At one of the short ends of the building, this area is flanked by a group of individual offices for executives, conference and other ancillary rooms as well as two minor open-plan office spaces. The lower floor has a reinforced concrete structure with mushroom-type columns spaced at 24'. This close spacing was acceptable as there was little need for flexibility for the facilities to be accommodated here.

Key elements in the open-plan offices are free-standing natural oak carrels with 5'8" high walls which, like the building itself, conform to a module of 6' × 6'.

The steel framework is painted black, forming a contrast to the bronze anodized aluminum window frames and to the grey granite used for the cladding of the base.

The steel framework of the upper floor is ▷ clearly distinguishable from the glass wall and from the upper part of the lower floor, visible below.

42

General view of the building. Only the upper floor seems to emerge from the ground.

Plans (lower floor, upper floor).
 1 Entrance lobby
 2 Open-plan office
 3 Open court
 4 Dining room
 5 Conference room
 6 Individual offices
 7 Data processing
 8 Mail room
 9 Stores
10 Mechanical equipment
11 Loading ramp

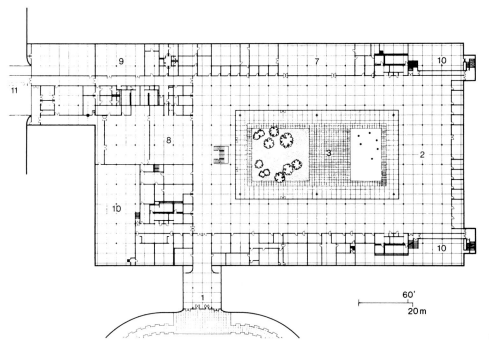

60'
20 m

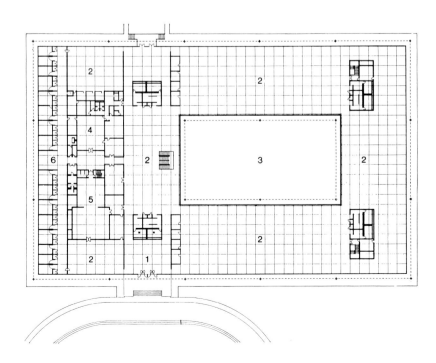

Interior court, seen from the main stairs.

The open-plan offices are furnished with freestanding natural oak carrels with 5'8" high walls. They conform to the same module as the building.

Corner of the building. The foundations of ▷ the outer steel columns are independent of the lower floor.

Training Center of the Eastman Kodak Company, Henrietta, New York

This group of buildings is designed to promote the advanced training of the technical and commercial members of the staff. It is located on an attractive rural site of 400 acres and has a total floor space of about 350,000 sq ft. It can accommodate 200 trainees at a time and has a permanent staff of 300.

The program specified a high degree of flexibility, with the possibility of altering one area without disturbing an adjacent area. The group consists of four buildings specially adapted for distinct functions; their building materials – weathering steel, brown brick and bronze tinted glass – as well as their size are designed to merge unobtrusively with the landscape.

Three of the buildings – laboratory, seminar and reception – are connected by service towers so as to form a single group while the fourth – a dining pavilion which is also formally distinguished by its curved walls – is self-contained though linked with the other buildings by a pedestrian subway.

The laboratory building has external corridors surrounding a central modular space which permits complete flexibility of use. Underfloor ducts connect the workplaces with a central core containing the service piping. The laboratory furniture conforms to the same module of $3' \times 3'$.

The seminar building contains external classroom zones with movable partitions governed by a module of $6' \times 6'$, and a central zone with permanently equipped lecture rooms. The four tiered seminar rooms on top are equipped with turntables which rotate the front walls. One lecture room on the lower level has a complete audio-visual equipment.

In the reception building are the administrative offices as well as the common rooms and studies of the teaching staff, and a library. The only fixed point in an otherwise open plan is a core with stairs, service rooms and installation shafts.

The main floor of the dining pavilion is spanned by a steel truss roof without intermediate columns. Roof structure and supporting brick walls are separated by small steel hinges.

Laboratory building, seen from northeast. In the ▷
background, right, part of the dining pavilion.

Plan (2nd floor) and section.
1 Reception building
2 Seminar building
3 Laboratory building
4 Dining pavilion

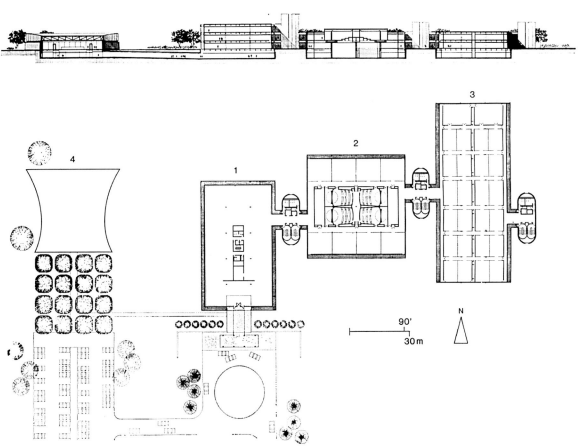

Seminar and reception buildings, seen from southeast.

Service tower between the laboratory and seminar buildings.

South side of the dining pavilion.

Seminar and laboratory buildings, seen from ▷ the forecourt of the reception building.

50

Boise Cascade Home Office, Boise, Idaho

The building is situated in the central business district of the city. To promote close contacts between departments and facilitate changes in organization, the company had insisted on an owner-occupied building with open-plan office accommodation. This resulted in a fairly compact volume of low profile, in keeping with the existing scale of the central business district. The building accommodates the 1,200 members of the headquarters staff whose number is not expected to rise so that extensions need not be envisaged within a foreseeable future.

The building covers an area of 260' × 260' and encloses, above ground, a court with an area of about 106' × 106'. The basement provides space for a computer center, mechanical equipments as well as a dispatching and receiving area accessible by a ramp. The ground floor is a pedestrian precinct open to the street, with the court serving as an entry loggia open on all four sides. Each of the five upper floors has a floor area of 56,000 sq ft. At the four corners are cores with toilets, fire exit stairs, storerooms and mains shafts; the intermediate space along the four sides is occupied by column-free open-plan spaces, used as offices on the 2nd, 3rd, 4th, and 6th floors while the 5th floor contains a cafeteria seating 250 persons as well as a fully equipped audio-visual center. Each floor is connected by bridges with the elevator core in the center of the court.

The building is planned on a 5'2" module and has a one-story concrete basement structure supporting a steel frame structure for the upper floors. The columns along the outer walls and facing the court have a spacing of 36'2" while the main girders have a span of 72'4". The facade is painted steel cladding with bronze tinted glass. The plastic skylights above the court are supported by an aluminum space frame.

General view from the south. The compact ▷ building occupies an entire street block. The ground floor is designed as a pedestrian precinct, open to the street.

Site plan. The covered court serves as an entry loggia. In its center are four elevator towers, connected by bridges with the upper floors.

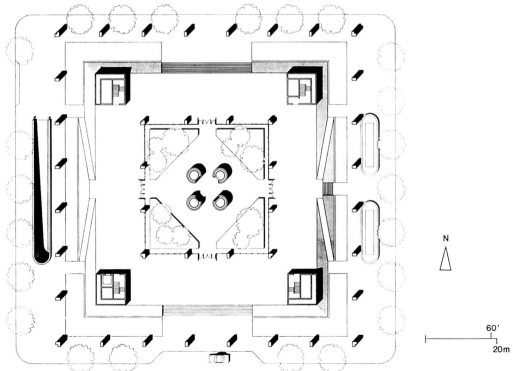

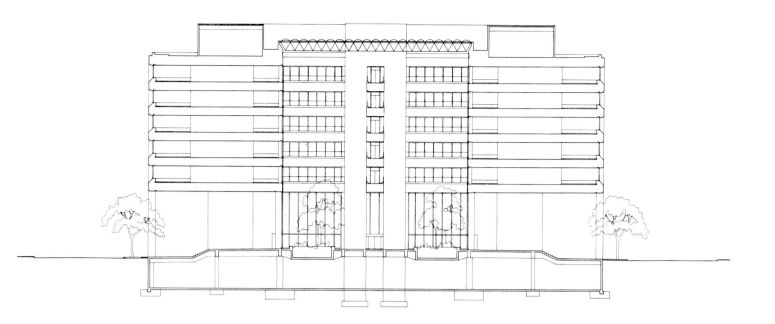

Plan of typical floor, and section.

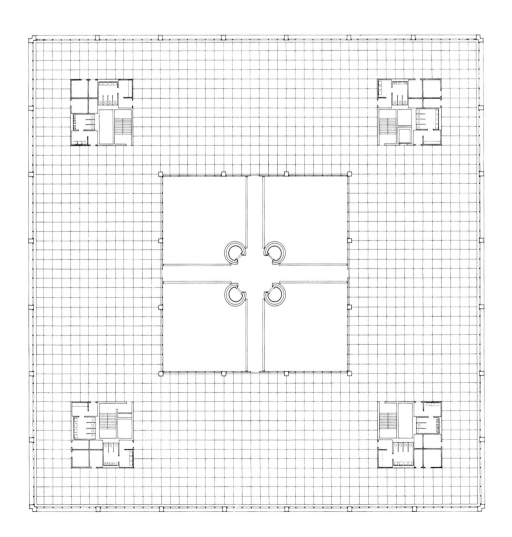

Views of the court. The four circular elevator towers form a lively contrast to the strictly orthogonal shapes of the main building.

Administrative and Research Headquarters of the Emhart Corporation, Bloomfield, Connecticut

The building occupies a site of 100 acres, has a total floor area of about 160,000 sq ft, and can accommodate 400 persons. The site adjoins that of the Connecticut General Life Insurance building, completed by Skidmore, Owings & Merrill in 1957. The two neighbors form a striking contrast. Connecticut General has non-fireproof steel structures with metal and glass curtain walls dominating the design, and surface parking, whereas Emhart is an early example of the use of exposed structural concrete with the more complex sculptural forms which that material permits, and the parking is virtually invisible both from within the building and from the approach.

The owner wished to have all his working departments on one level and this led to planning the office space around the upper part of a higher pilot laboratory. Because of the terrain it was possible to put the laboratory and its service access at grade and carry the surrounding office floor on concrete trees so that it rides majestically across the spine of the ridge which is the principal feature of the site. Beneath this horizontal umbrella is the parking, some open and some in a basement garage beneath an entrance court. This court leads to a lobby in the very center of the building giving access to the main floor from below by a stairway. Suspended from the concrete soffit is a cafeteria which rides over the parking and affords a dramatic view of the adjacent valley.

The predominant element of the design is the concrete structure. The cantilevered trees, spaced 42' apart, consist of ribbed columns whose ribs are extended to produce a vaulted design for the soffit. At the corners of the square trees are fireproofed steel columns on the inside and precast concrete columns on the perimeter, the latter being separated by hinges from the steel roof.

The low white concrete structure, accentuated by the dark recessed glass wall behind, dominates the top of the hill and the concealment of the parking was a pivotal step in the handling of this recurrent contemporary problem.

A view of the court from the zone facing the ▷ main entrance.

Site plan. Top, right: Part of the building of the Connecticut General Life Insurance Co.

Pages 58–59:
General view of the building from the south.
The main floor with the administrative offices rides majestically across the flat ridge.

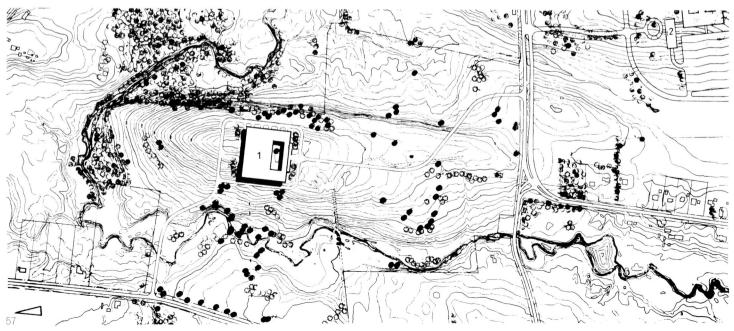

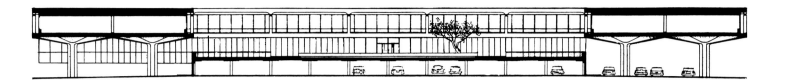

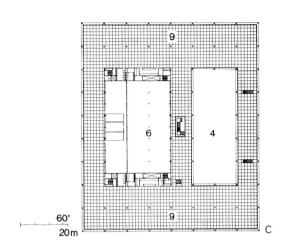

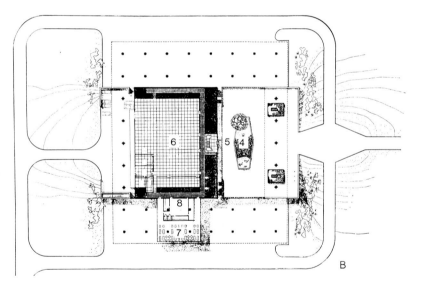

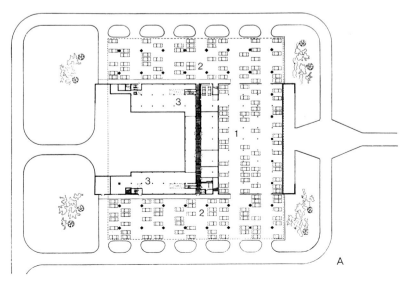

Plans and section across the court looking
toward main entrance.
A Ground level
B Entrance floor
C Main floor
1 Garage
2 Parking
3 Service rooms
4 Court
5 Main entrance
6 Laboratory
7 Cafeteria
8 Kitchen
9 Office area

Corner of cantilevered main floor. ▷

**Headquarters of the General Reinsurance Company, Greenwich, Connecticut.
Under construction**

The plot is situated directly adjacent to Greenwich harbor. To enable the greatest possible number of staff to enjoy the fine view, it was decided to give the building a long and narrow shape, parallel to the water's edge.

The parking garage, accommodating some 450 cars, is on two basement levels; one of these is completely below ground, while the other is contained below two grassplanted terraces which are sloped at the edges. The terraces are interrupted by a wide passage which, even from the road, provides a view of the bay. It is at this passage that the main entrances with lobbies for visitors and guests are situated. The upper part of the building comprises three floors which are divided into three units by pairs of recessed service cores. These contain stairs, elevators, toilets and miscellaneous storage areas and – in the top part which over-towers the main block by nearly 17' – the elevator machinery, heating and air-conditioning plant. The areas in the three units separated by the cores cover about 145' × 85' each and are interrupted by only four columns. At terrace level, the two units at the ends contain cafeteria and other areas with direct access to the outsides; all the other areas – totalling some 165,000 sq ft – contain offices. The ceilings which, like the other parts of the bearing structure, consist of concrete have a waffle pattern governed by a 5' × 5' module. They are left exposed, and their recessed spaces contain the light fixtures. The bronze tinted windows, set back by one module, extend from floor to ceiling so that the framework structure is clearly visible.

It is planned to landscape the site with more than eighty new trees.

Facade detail (model). The glass walls are set ▷
back by one row of waffle ceiling units from
the outer edge of the building so that the
framework structure is clearly visible.

General view from the west (model).

Plan (typical floor).
1 Office area
2 Core
3 Passage
4 Terrace
5 Water

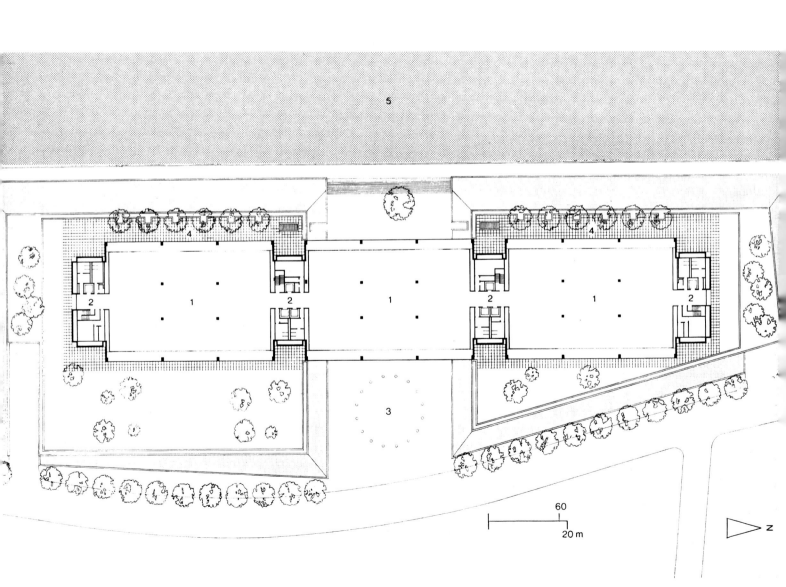

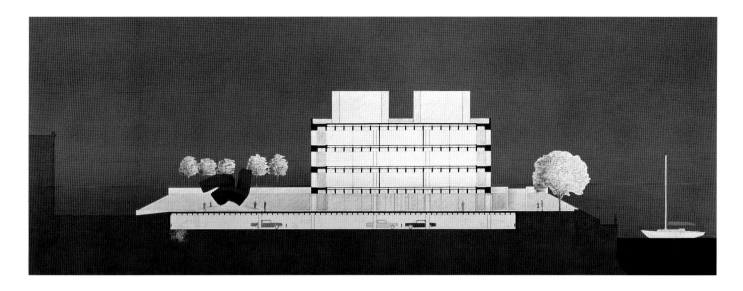

Cross-section at the passage.

Model, seen from above.

Headquarters of the American Can Company, Greenwich, Connecticut

The buildings have been placed on an estate of 175 acres in such a way that they remain concealed from the residential area in the southeast. They comprise a podium with garage accommodation for 1,700 cars and ancillary facilities, a general administration building, and a smaller single-story building for the executive offices.

The podium bridges a small ravine, acting as a dam and thereby creating a lake on the upstream side from which the flow of water to a swampy bird sanctuary along the southwest border of the estate can be regulated. The cafeteria is on the top floor of the podium, with a terrace overlooking the lake.

The main building above the podium covers an area of 525' × 255' and contains, on its three levels, a total office floor area of 558,422 sq ft. The inside areas are mainly used as open-plan offices, with individual offices along the periphery. The structural bays measure 30' × 60'. The structure consists of a poured-in-place reinforced concrete framework with twin girders, supporting precast double-web ceiling beams placed longitudinally. The tubes suspended between the webs, which have the treble function of carrying the light fixtures, acting as sound absorbers and serving as air ducts, represent a variation of an idea used first at the headquarters of the American Republic Insurance Company, Des Moines (pages 94–101). But while in Des Moines, the air is diffused and returned at the bottom of the tube, the openings are, in the present building, on top of the tube on either side of the light fixture.

The smaller executive building has but one story, covering an area of 165' × 165'. Because of the larger bays of 60' × 60', the girders are here of one piece, and are prestressed. In contrast to the main building, the roof structure is concealed inside behind a continuous suspended ceiling.

Site plan.
1 General administration building
2 Executive offices

View of the general administration building ▷ from southeast, with the highway in the foreground.

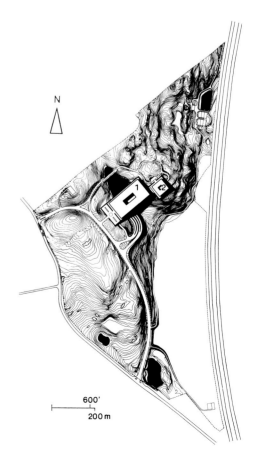

N

600'
200 m

View of the buildings from the west, with visitors' parking in the foreground.

View of the buildings from the south. Each floor of the garage has its own access ramp.

Cross-section and longitudinal section of the main building.

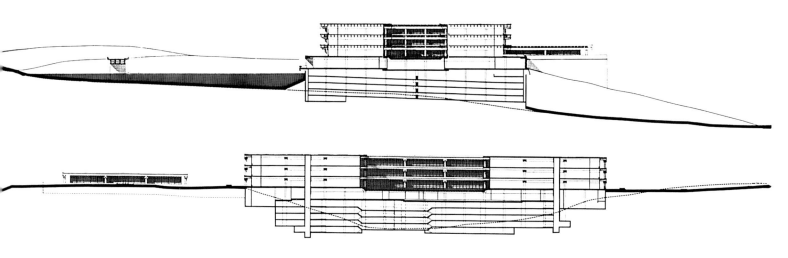

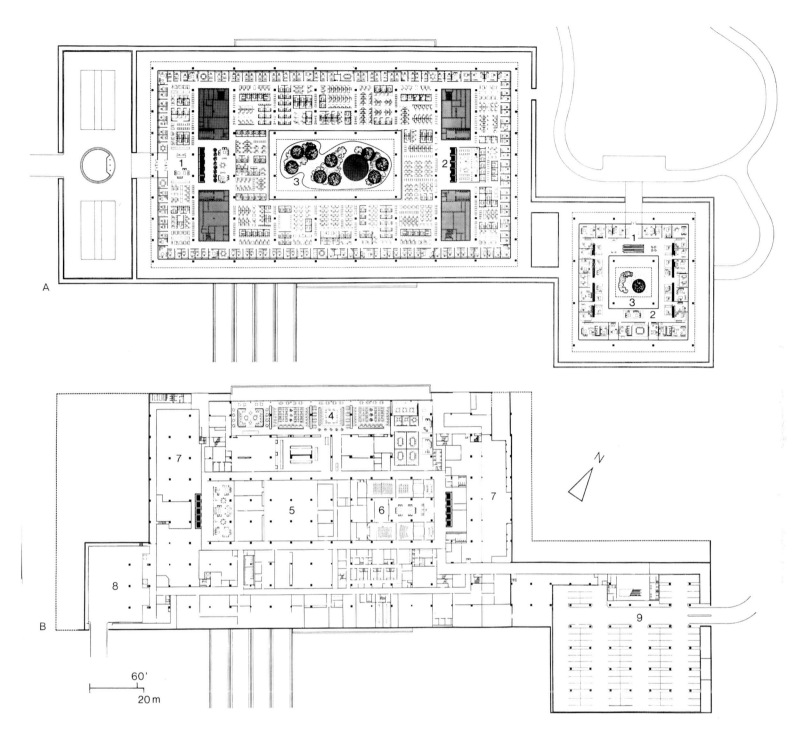

Plans.

A Top floor of podium

B Ground floor

1 Entrance lobby

2 Offices

3 Central court

4 Cafeteria

5 Data processing center

6 Training center

7 Mechanical equipment

8 Loading dock

9 Executive garage

Pages 70–71:

View from the north. On the left, the single-story executive building; on the right, the general administration building.

60'

20 m

N

A

B

Central court in the executive building. The tree was brought in by helicopter.

Corner of the executive building. The caps of the tensioning cables in the main girders are of stainless steel.

The executive building, seen from the north, with the entrance to its garage on the left.

Waiting area in the executive building.

View from the cafeteria over the artificial lake toward the bridge carrying the access road to the executive building.

General administration building, seen from across the lake.

Corner of the general administration building. ▷ The bearing structure consists of a framework of poured-in-place sandblasted reinforced concrete and precast double-web floor units.

Headquarters of the Weyerhaeuser Company, Tacoma, Washington

The building occupies a site about midway between Tacoma and the Seattle-Tacoma Airport. The dominant feature of the site is a shallow valley, running north to south.
The building is placed like a dam across the valley and its five floors are stepped back on the long sides so that each successive floor is narrower than the one below. In the three lower floors are the general offices. The next floor is level with the ridges on either side of the valley and contains the main entrances, a cafeteria, a small lecture room and employees' lounge. On the narrowest 5th floor are the executive offices.
The architects' guiding idea had been to create a building which would "literally tend to disappear – becoming one with the landscape." All the roof surfaces are gently sloped and are, except for the 5th floor, covered with ivy. The windows are hardly apparent as they are deeply recessed behind the roof edges and are, moreover, not interrupted by any vertical dividers which might impair the visual merger between interior and exterior.
Even in the design of the offices, the architects were guided by the principle of undefined boundaries. There are no full-height interior partitions and the different departments merge imperceptibly. The endeavor to create open office landscapes is also emphasized by the placing of the columns which is governed by a diamond-shaped grid turned at an angle to the basic rectangle of the building.
The structure of the building is a concrete-clad steel frame. Much of the interior wood-work was produced in the workshops of the company which is one of the leading manu-facturers of wood products.
The landscape architects were Sasaki, Walker Associates.

Site plan. The building is placed like a dam ▷
across a valley, and both its long sides are
stepped back from bottom to top floor.

Pages 78–79:
View of the eastern main entrance at 4th-floor
level.

N

600'

200 m

General view of the building. On the north side, the valley has been converted into a small lake.

Plans and sections ▷
A Ground floor
B 2nd floor
C 3rd floor
D 4th floor
E 5th floor
1 Office area
2 Service core
3 Mechanical equipment
4 Incoming goods
5 Car parks
6 Main entrance
7 Elevator lobby
8 Lounge
9 Cafeteria
10 Lecture room

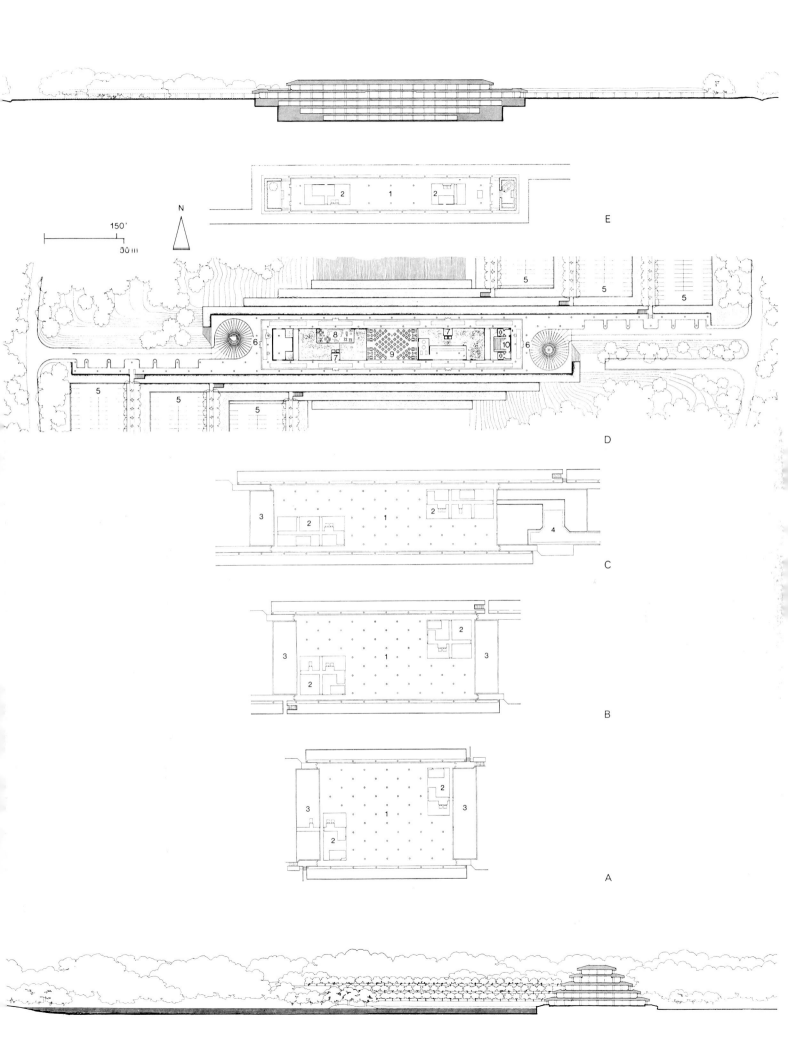

D

C

B

A

N

150'

30 m

Like the three lower floors, the 5th floor with the executive offices is designed as an "office landscape."

View of one of the two long side corridors on
the 4th floor.

Conversation group at one end of the central
expanse on the 5th floor. The tapestry is by
Helena Hernmarck.

Office of the company's president in the central expanse on the 5th floor.

The cafeteria on the 4th floor.

Cashier's station and condiment stands. On ▷
the left, the access to the cafeteria.

Banque Lambert, Brussels

The building faces the Avenue Marnix which is part of the inner ring of boulevards surrounding the town center and is opposite the Royal Palace. It has nine stories above two basements.

The basements occupy the whole site and contain the bank vault, an employees' cafeteria, mechanical equipment and a garage for 120 cars. The ground floor is recessed from the facades above and contains the entrance lobbies and banking hall. Above the ground floor are seven typical office floors which can be flexibly subdivided as open areas or private offices. The top floor is again set back and contains the apartment of the Lambert family as well as a suite of rooms for conference and entertaining. The plan of the typical floors, which cover an area of 100' × 240', is based on a module of 4'6" × 4'6". A central service core contains elevators, stairs, toilets and mechanical shafts.

The bearing structure of the building is of reinforced concrete. The ribbed floor slabs are supported at the inside by columns along the lines of the walls of the central core and, at the outer perimeter, by cross-shaped precast concrete units which form the facades outside the glass walls. These units are one module wide and one story high, with half units top and bottom. The vertical legs join half-way between floors where the load is transmitted through polished steel ball-and-socket hinge joints cast integrally with the crosses. At the ground floor ceiling, the perimeter loads are transmitted by a floor beam to columns set back from the facades and spaced 31'6" apart.

The vertical legs of the load-bearing cross-shaped facade units join at polished steel hinge joints embedded in the concrete.

Southwest corner of the plaza with Henry ▷
Moore's sculpture "Locking Piece."   88

Plans and section.

A Entrance floor
B Typical floor
C Penthouse floor
1 Entrance lobby
2 Banking hall
3 Offices open to the public
4 Typical offices
5 Ballroom
6 Executive dining room
7 Drawing room
8 Gallery
9 Library
10 Bedroom
11 Guest room
12 Private dining room
13 Kitchen
14 Servants' lounge

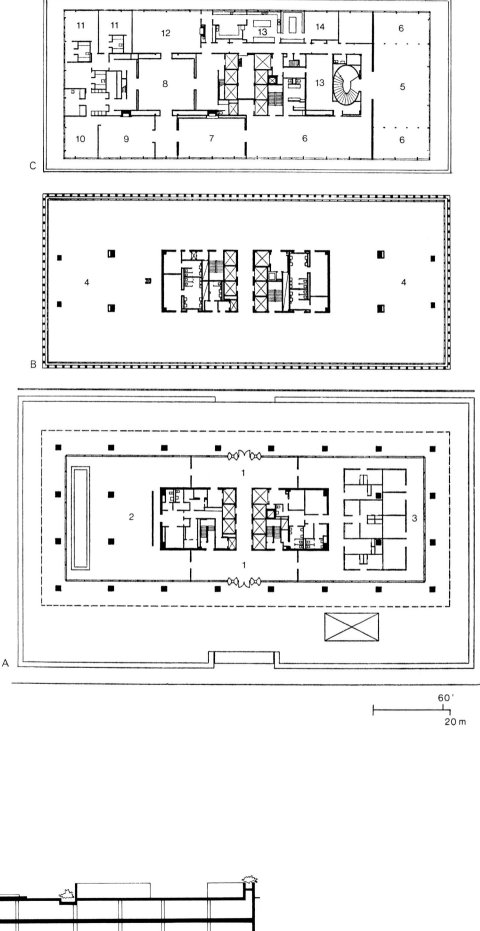

60'

20 m

General view of the building from northwest,
with the Avenue Marnix in the foreground.

Baron Lambert's office.

Executive dining room in the penthouse.

Baron Lambert's library, with drawing room and executive dining room in the background.

Gallery in the center of the penthouse apart- ▷
ment. In the foreground a sculpture by Giaco-
metti; next to the passage a Baga figure; in
the room between drawing room and library
a sculpture by Ipousteguy. Daylight enters
through plastic domes in the roof. Floor slabs
are of travertine; the walls are plastered.

Headquarters of the American Republic Insurance Company, Des Moines, Iowa

The building is located on a narrow site sloping from north to south on the periphery of the central business district, and can accommodate 650 people. It consists of a six-story office tower above an enclosed podium which projects to the south around an entrance courtyard. Podium and tower are independent both structurally and visually, merely sharing a common central core which stiffens the entire structure. To emphasize the suspension of the upper block the one-story space between it and the podium is enclosed with continuous glass and contains the cafeteria and a lounge opening on to a terrace overlooking the entrance court. The load-bearing walls on the east and west of the tower are of poured-in-place reinforced concrete with a selected granite aggregate which is sandblasted. They are about 180′ long and taper from 4′ at the bottom to 21″ at the top as the loads diminish. The wall loads are transmitted to four concrete columns on either side, which are totally free of the podium, by story-high steel hinges painted black which punctuate the cafeteria level. The floors of the tower are of prestressed precast tees with a span of 98′ and these are smooth-finished in contrast to the rough texture of the sandblasted walls. The north and south walls are of floor to ceiling gray glass deeply recessed.

The ceiling system represents a complete integration of structural and mechanical elements. Between the structural tees are tubes covered with acoustical material which alternate as supply and return air ducts: above the tubes are placed very high intensity fluorescent lights which are fully concealed from the observer. The result is a uniform distribution of indirect light, conditioned air and sound absorption within the framework of the exposed structure.

All the details are carefully attuned to the basic structural concept. The architectural effect is handsomely complemented by works of art by contemporary artists, including a specially commissioned stabile by Alexander Calder in the entrance court and a Corbusier tapestry in the chairman's office on the top floor.

Corner of the building. The walls and columns ▷ of sandblasted exposed concrete, the smooth prestressed concrete members, the black painted steel hinges and the aluminum-framed windows create a lively contrast.

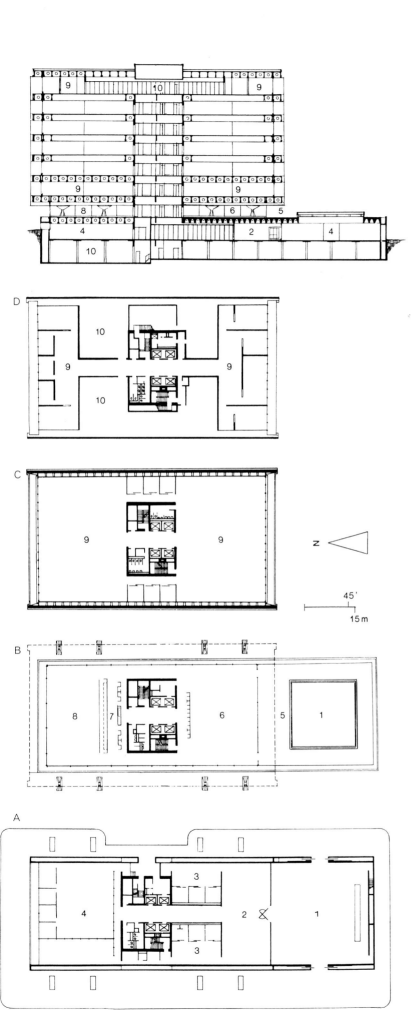

Plans and longitudinal section.
A Ground floor
B Mezzanine
C Typical floor
D Executive floor
1 Entrance court
2 Lobby
3 Visitors' offices
4 Computer area
5 Terrace
6 Lounge
7 Food service
8 Cafeteria
9 Offices
10 Mechanical equipment

Views from northeast. As the load-bearing walls taper towards the upper floors while the perimeter partitions remain in the same vertical alignment, the intermediate space available for the ducting decreases from top to bottom in keeping with the technical requirements – the air-conditioning plant being installed on the top floor.

Pages 98–99:
Employees' lounge. In the background, two of the black painted steel hinges.

96

West-side access to entrance court.

Entrance court, seen from the lobby.

Office area. The metal tubes suspended ▷ between the stems of the T-beams have the multiple function of diffusing the light of the fluorescent light fixtures mounted above them, acting as sound-absorbing elements with perforated cover and inside fiberglass insulation, and serving alternately as ducts for supply and return air.

Detail section of a structural floor in the office tower.
1 Prestressed concrete T-beam
2 Stiffener
3 Flooring
4 Carpeting
5 Air duct, also serving as sound-absorber
6 Fluorescent light fixture

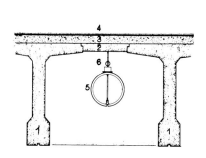

Cross-section of air duct/acoustic unit.
1 Hanger rod
2 Perforated aluminum tube
3 Sound-absorbing coating
4 Cover
5 Air supply or return diffuser
6 Base of fluorescent light fixture
7 Fluorescent light fixture

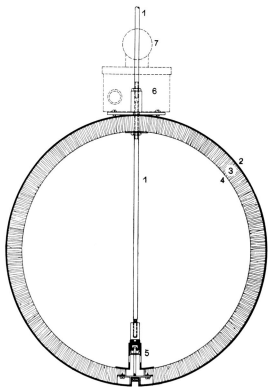

Air supply or return diffuser.
1 Aperture leading to air duct
2 Aperture leading to office space

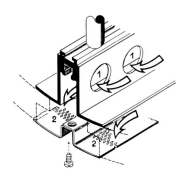

Headquarters of the Business Men's Assurance Co. of America, Kansas City, Missouri

The building is situated outside the city on a hill at the edge of a park. In addition to the 19-story tower, both a lower tower and a one- or two-story structure had been considered. The lower tower, however, would have had an unfavorable proportion with relation to the hill while the low-rise structure would have had to occupy nearly all of the 7-acre site to provide equivalent area.

The tower stands on a large platform. Below this platform are parking facilities, mechanical and other ancillary rooms as well as a cafeteria. The bearing structure is a frame of continuously welded high-strength steel with a column spacing of 36′ × 36′. Because of the frequent tornadoes experienced in this region, wind bracing had to be particularly strong, allowing for a maximum sway of about 5″ at the top. Cladding is of white Georgia marble.

The interior is developed on a 6′ × 6′ module. The window walls of gray, heat-absorbent glass, set back by one module, are held in black anodized aluminum frames. Behind every other window mullion is an air-conditioning duct leading to induction units on typical floors and low sill diffusers on the two top floors.

The building is situated on a hill adjacent to a ▷ park outside the city.

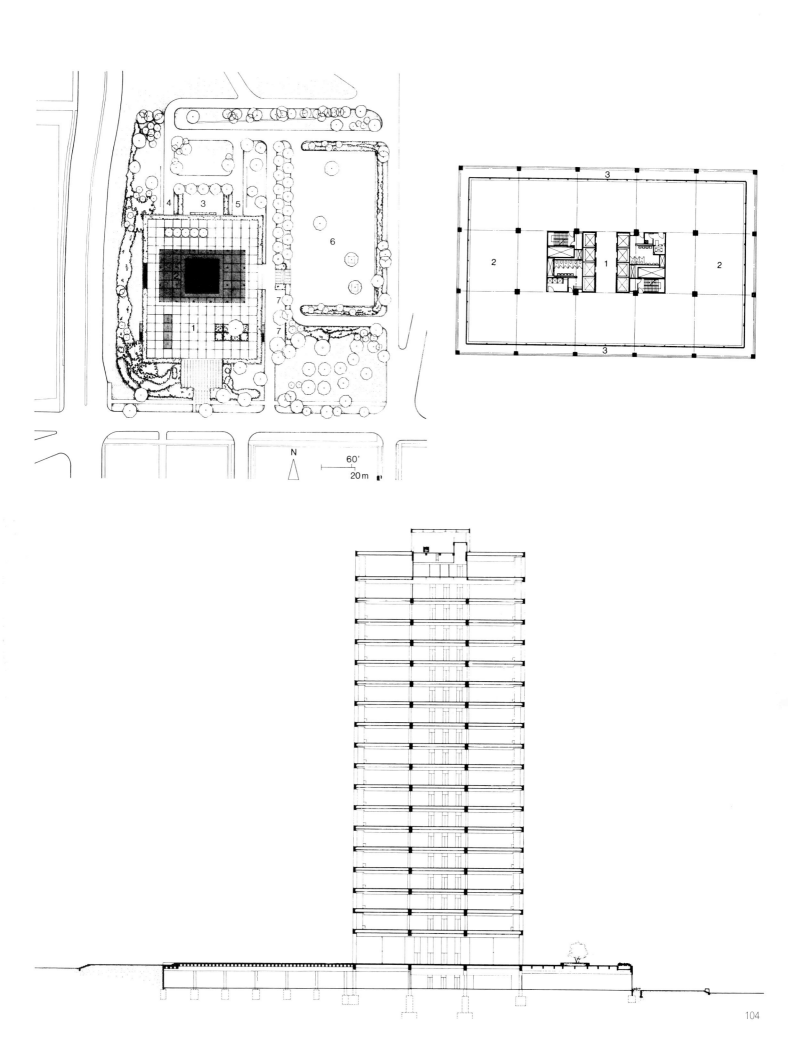

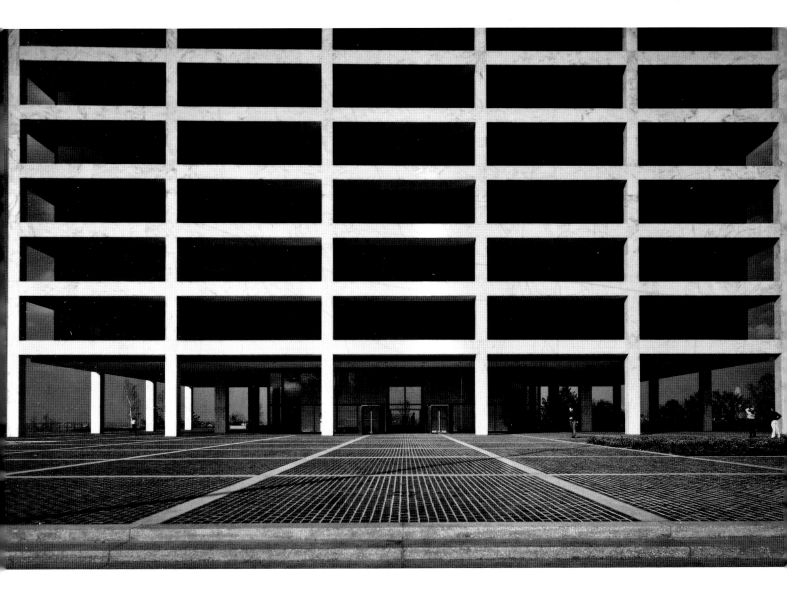

South side of the building. The structural frame, clad in white marble, is impressively distinguished from the recessed walls of gray, heat-absorbent glass.

◁ Site plan.
1 Terrace
2 Tower
3 Cafeteria terrace
4 Garage entrance drive
5 Supplies
6 Staff parking
7 Visitors' parking

Plan (ground floor).
1 Elevator lobby
2 Office space
3 Surrounding gallery

Section.

Tenneco Building, Houston, Texas

The building, headquarters of the Tennessee Gas Transmission Co. and the Tennessee Bank and Trust Co., stands in the center of a square block in the central business district of Houston. It covers an area of 195'4" × 195'4" with a total effective floor area of 907,190 sq ft, including some 845,320 sq ft on the 28 typical floors.

The comparatively low ground floor core is set back about 42'8" on all sides from the outside of the building so that, despite the high plot ratio, a spacious plaza has been created. The plaza is flanked by car ramps on two opposite sides and by five semi-circular drive-in tellers' booths on one of the two other sides. The two-story bank premises above the ground floor are likewise set back from the outside of the building, though by about 15'2" only. On the 28 typical floors, office space which can be partitioned at will is available on a module of 5'6" × 5'6" over a depth of 48' between the centrally placed core and the window walls. As the orientation of the building is such that each of the four sides is liable to be exposed to the sun at some time during the day, the window walls of the typical floors are set back by 6' from the spandrel line. Further protection against the hot southern sun is provided by sun screens suspended from the edge beams. The deep set-back of the first three floors is repeated at the top of the building where the lower part of the mechanical floor is also deeply recessed.

The bearing structure of the tower consists of a concrete-clad steel framework and steel floor units. The two-story bank premises above the ground floor are suspended from the nethermost typical floor by means of bars in the curtain wall. The cladding is "amber gray" anodized aluminum which has also been used for the window frames. The window panes are gray tinted.

The ground floor and the bank premises above it are set back so as to widen the plaza.

The lower parts of the external columns are reinforced. In the foreground, the semi-circular drive-in tellers' booths.

General view of the building. ▷

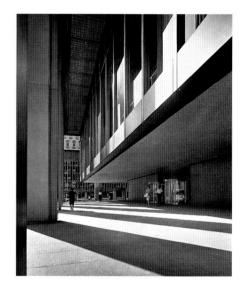

Corner of the building. The plaza is paved with Texas red granite.

Section of the facade at typical floor level. Because of Houston's southern climate, the glass wall is set back 6' from the spandrel line, and sun screens are suspended from the edge beams.

With its dark cladding and agreeable proportions, ▷ the building has a distinguished appearance.

Plans (ground floor, typical floor).
1 Plaza
2 Lobby
3 Drive-in tellers' booths
4 Car ramp
5 Office area, capable of being partitioned at will

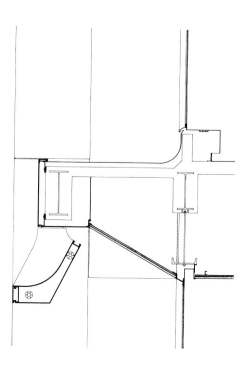

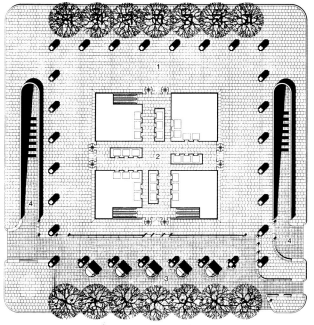

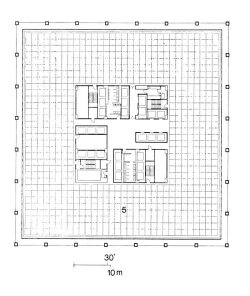

30'
10 m

Carlton Centre, Johannesburg, South Africa

Carlton Centre, designed jointly by Skidmore, Owings & Merrill and W. Rhodes-Harrison, Hoffe and Partners was the first major redevelopment of a portion of downtown Johannesburg, and has served as a catalyst for other developments.

Four small city blocks, characteristic of the basic city structure which dates back to the time when it was little more than a miners' camp, were incorporated into one "superblock" by closing portions of two intersecting streets. Parts of two other blocks were also developed concurrently on the south side of Main Street. A 50-story office building, a 600-room luxury hotel, and a department store, the main architectural elements of the complex, are grouped around a large circular court which penetrates the two shopping levels below the plaza. Much of the street level is therefore left open for pedestrians, landscaped areas, open courts and entrances to the shopping levels.

South of Main Street, a large rectangular structure contains a department store and shops at street level and on two levels below the street, 6 floors of parking and at the top a column-free exhibition hall. The two lower shopping levels are joined beneath Main Street to the major shopping concourses below the plaza. 140 retail shops, restaurants and banks are thus connected by covered malls, providing shoppers with a traffic-free, all-weather shopping complex connected vertically by escalators and elevators to the major buildings as well as to parking spaces for more than 2,000 cars both below and above street level. A service level immediately below the shopping concourse is reserved exclusively for the delivery of goods.

The entire complex is designed in poured-in-place reinforced concrete and all structures above grade have an integral finish of local gray granite exposed by sandblasting. The total area of the project is approximately 3,500,000 sq ft.

Carlton Centre, viewed from the southeast. ▷
In the left foreground, the Carlton Exhibition
Centre; beyond it the Carlton Hotel; in the
background the 50-story office tower.

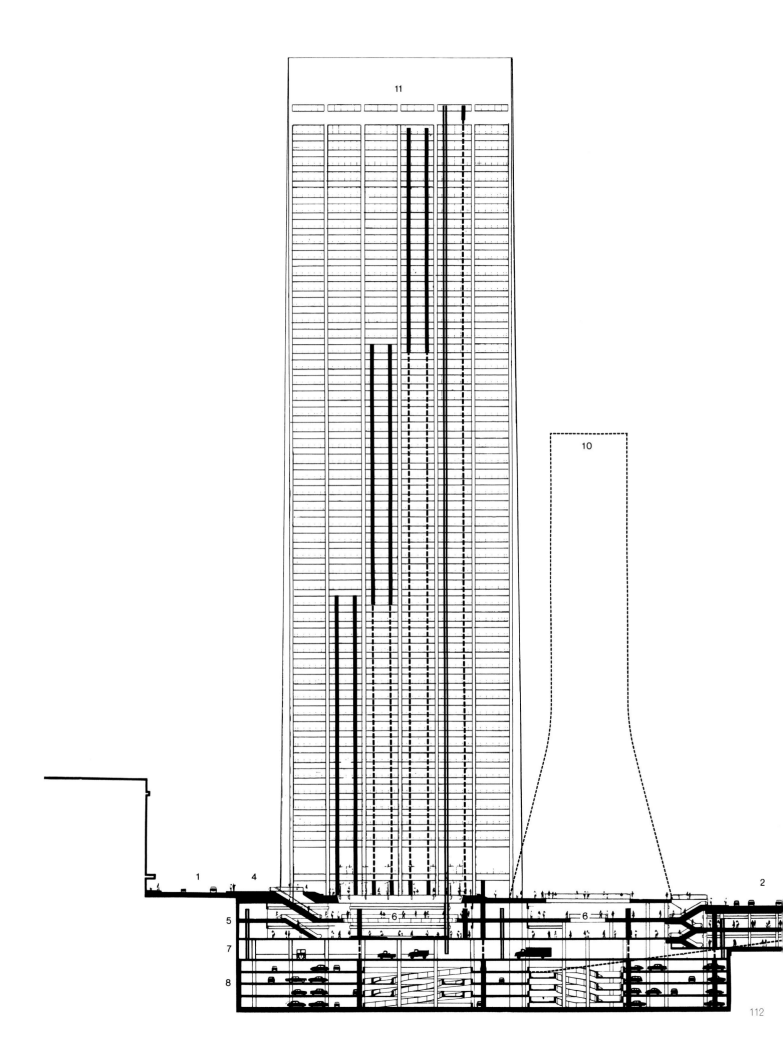

Section.
1 Commissioner Street
2 Main Street
3 Marshall Street
4 Plaza
5 Shops
6 Court
7 Delivery level
8 Parking
9 Exhibition hall
10 Hotel
11 Office tower

Plans.
A First basement
B Plaza level
1 Commissioner Street
2 Main Street
3 Marshall Street
4 Kruis Street
5 Von Wielligh Street
6 Plaza
7 Court
8 Department store
9 Retail shops
10 Hotel
11 Office tower

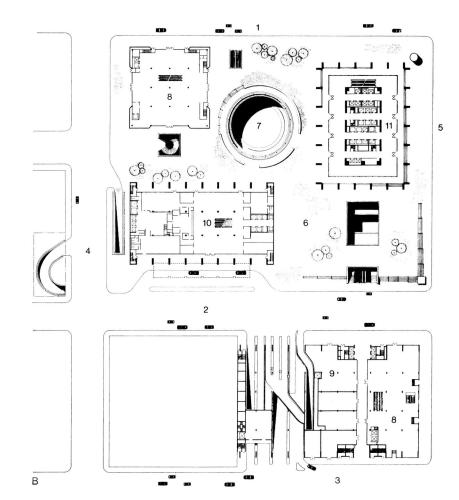

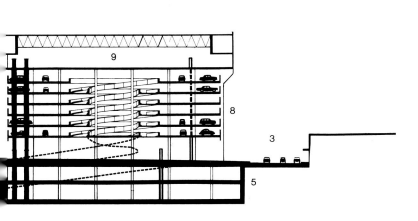

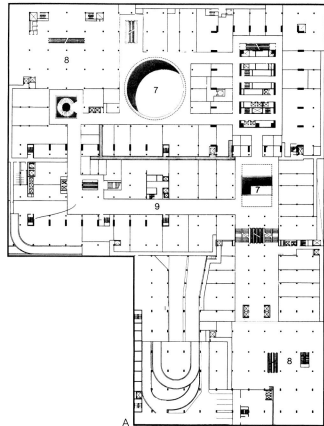

The large circular court is a central feature of the plaza. It provides a visual link between the shopping levels and the street. Ice-skating in the winter and a large fountain in the summer are added attractions.

The Carlton Exhibition Centre, with shops at the ground floor and two basement levels, six levels of parking and an exhibition hall at the top.

Office building and the hotel. The lower ▷ portions of the hotel become wider to accommodate special suites, function rooms, a ballroom, restaurants and other public areas.

Bank of America Headquarters, San Francisco, California

The complex – a joint venture of Skidmore, Owings & Merrill and Wurster, Bernardi and Emmons with Pietro Belluschi as consulting architect – consists of a 52-story tower, a pavilion with ground floor and galleries on two levels, and a four-level base.

The tower was placed at the extreme southwest corner and the pavilion at the extreme northeast corner of the site, leaving about 50 percent of the site free for a large plaza along California Street on the north side.

The level immediately below the plaza contains a pedestrian concourse with entrances from three streets. Here are a cafeteria, an auditorium with 220 seats, as well as shops. Below that level are truck delivery and pick-up facilities and a three-level basement garage for 420 cars.

The pavilion, containing the San Francisco main office branch of the bank, is supported by four robust corner columns. The two gallery levels and the ground floor, accessible from Montgomery Street on the east side, offer a total floor area of 30,000 sq ft.

The tower, covering an area of 143′ × 243′ in the plan, contains a total floor area of 1,600,000 sq ft. The bank occupies about one-third of the office space, the remainder being available for tenancy by other firms. To improve the sculptural quality of the 779′ high tower, a bay window design has been adopted for the facades, and the upper floors are distinguished by irregular setbacks. The facades are composed of polished granite of a reddish color, and of bronze tinted glass. While, on the standard floors, the windows point outwards and the columns are merged with the inside window posts, giving the appearance of a smooth skin which does not conceal the plastic shape of the building, the windows of the banking hall on the 2nd and 3rd floors point inwards so as to emphasize the columns and to preserve formal continuity with the recessed main lobby on the ground floor.

Section. On the left, the glass pavilion with the San Francisco main office branch of the bank.

The tower, seen from the north. The facade ▷ is enlivened by a bay window pattern and the upper floors by irregular setbacks.

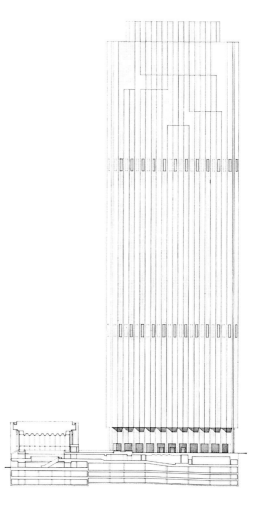

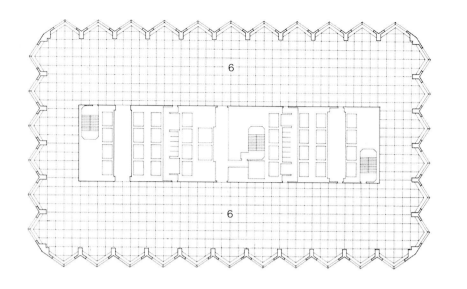

Plans (plaza level, standard office floor).
1 Plaza
2 Fountain
3 Sculpture
4 Pavilion
5 Main lobby of office tower
6 Office space
7 California commercial union building

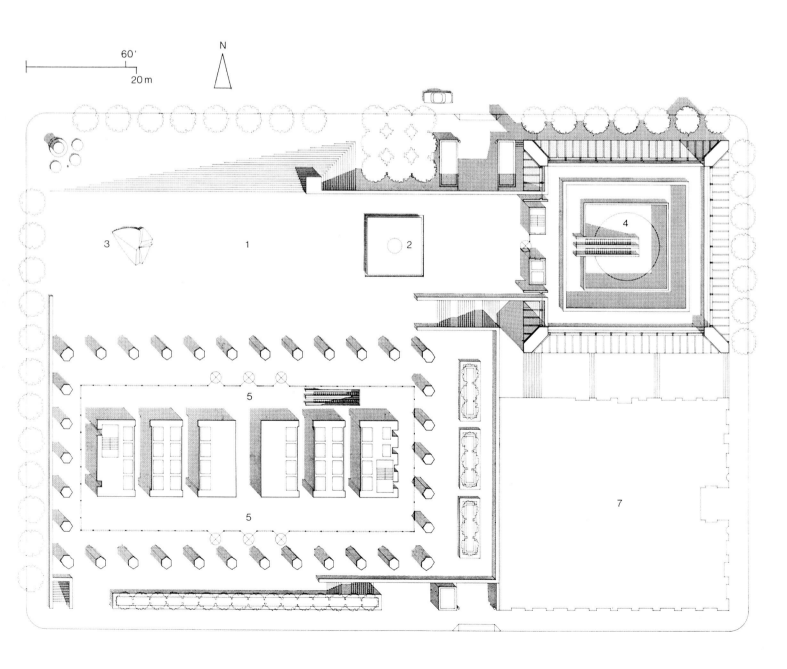

60'
20 m

N

Office with view across the San Francisco Bay.

Interior of the two-story banking hall in the tower.

The pavilion, seen from the west.

◁ Plaza, adjoining California Street.

Interior of the pavilion. Northeast corner of the
building, seen from the upper gallery.

Marine Midland Center, Buffalo, New York. Under construction

The site earmarked for this office block, designed for rental, covers two street blocks in the central business district. The phase I project includes a 40-story tower, bridging Main Street and covering an area of 120′ × 160′, as well as an L-shaped ancillary building which flanks the tower on the south and west sides, with the south wing likewise bridging the street. Total floor area is about 1,400,000 sq ft. Some 82 percent of the office space is available to the principal tenants (Marine Midland Bank) for their own purposes or for subletting.

The two basements contain a garage accommodating 550 cars, which is wholly owned and operated by the City of Buffalo, as well as the bank's computer center and storage and mechanical areas. At the level of Main Street is a spacious plaza, enlivened by regularly spaced flower boxes with honey locust trees and by a large sculpture piece. Pedestrian access to the tower is from lobbies on either side of Main Street. Primary access to the ancillary building is placed at the intersection of its two wings. The ground floor of its south wing contains a branch bank; in the west wing are a restaurant and shops; from the entrance lobbies on either side of Main Street, escalators lead to a two-story high main lobby which is also the bottom landing for most of the elevators serving the upper floors of the tower. A bridge, approximately 90′ wide, connects the lobby with the south wing of the ancillary building which, at that level, contains an auditorium and a cafeteria. The executive dining rooms are on the top floor of the tower.

The buildings are clad in chamfered precast concrete panels, 4″ in thickness, finished with washed silicate gravel. The window ribbons have bronze tinted glass panes with dark anodized aluminum frames.

The group of buildings, seen from the north ▷
(model).

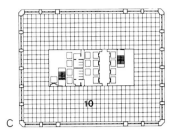

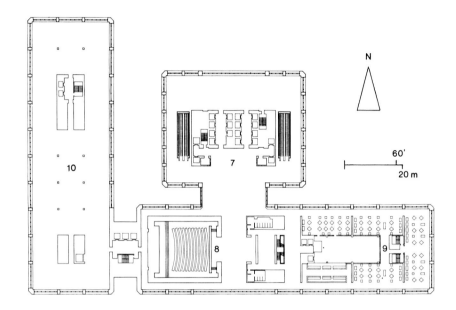

C 10

B 10   7

N

60'
20 m

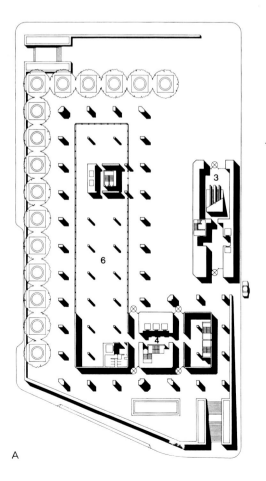

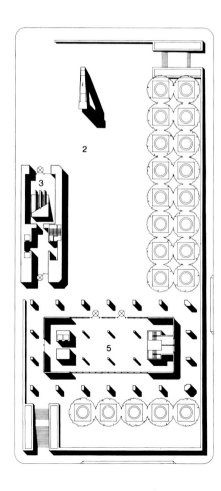

A

1   2

3   3

6   5

4

Plans.
A Ground floor
B 2nd floor
C Typical floor of the tower
1 Main Street
2 Plaza
3 Tower entrance lobby
4 Lobby of ancillary building
5 Banking area
6 Restaurant and shops
7 Main lobby of tower
8 Auditorium
9 Cafeteria
10 Office space

View from above on the northern part of ▷
the plaza (model).   124

Marine Midland Building, New York, New York

The Marine Midland Building was the first New York office building designed by Skidmore, Owings & Merrill as a commercial building for general rental, which has somewhat different demands from those of a corporate headquarters. It occupies a small site in the Wall Street area in the immediate vicinity of the Chase Manhattan Bank, completed in 1961.

As it was desired to leave as much open space as possible facing Broadway and Cedar Street without, however, voluntarily forgoing the maximum permissible plot ratio on this very costly site, the setback from the two other streets had to be reduced to the minimum permitted by the 1961 zoning ordinance. The building was therefore given the same trapezoidal shape as the site itself which entailed, however, hardly any disadvantages compared with a rectangular plan as the odd angles could be absorbed in the likewise trapezoidal central core so that the number of critical points could be reduced to a minimum.

The major tenant, for whom the building is named, is the Marine Midland Grace Trust Company (now the Marine Midland Bank). This bank occupies the two basements which cover the entire site, as well as the first ten floors above street level. The main banking hall is placed on the 2nd floor while the ground floor had to be reserved for general facilities available to all the tenants, particularly the main lobby.

The bearing structure of the tower is a welded steel frame, with approximately 30' × 30' bays. Because of the irregular angles, the architects opted for a smooth facade clad with a uniform skin of mat-black anodized aluminum and bronze tinted glass, emphasizing the structure as a whole while repressing the individual elements.

The sculpture on the plaza facing Broadway, a red painted rhombohedron 28' high, was designed by Isamu Noguchi in collaboration with Skidmore, Owings & Merrill.

Site plan.
1 Broadway
2 Cedar Street
3 Liberty Street
4 Nassau Street
5 Pine Street
6 William Street
7 Marine Midland Building
8 Chase Manhattan Bank

Northwest side of the building, with Isamu ▷ Noguchi's sculpture in the foreground.

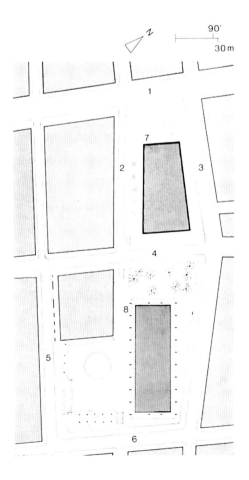

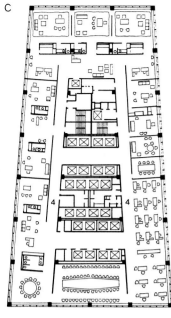

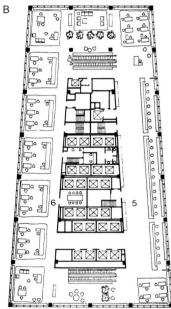

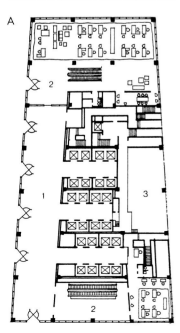

C

B

A

Plans.
A Ground floor
B 2nd floor
C 3rd floor
1 Entrance lobby
2 Bank premises
3 Truck dock
4 Offices
5 Banking hall
6 Officers' platform

Facade detail.
1 Corner column
2 Edge beam
3 Steel deck floor with concrete cover
4 Fireproofing
5 Concrete block
6 Aluminum panel
7 Guide rail for window washing rig
8 Glass
9 Metal lath and plaster
10 Suspended ceiling
11 Cladding of induction unit

Page 129: ▷
The smooth facade of mat-black anodized aluminum and bronze tinted glass has the effect of emphasizing the shape as a whole and subordinating the individual elements.

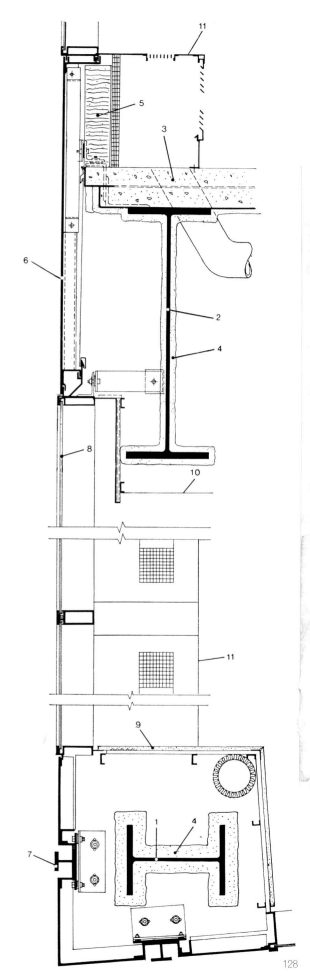

◁ View of the building from west with the Chase
Manhattan Bank in the background.

131   Banking hall on the 2nd floor.

U.S. Steel Building, One Liberty Plaza, New York, New York

The building is situated between Broadway, Liberty, Church and Cortlandt Streets. To the west is the World Trade Center; to the east, the Marine Midland Building which was also designed by SOM.

U.S. Steel, joint owner with Galbreath-Ruffin Corporation, requested a tower clearly expressing the steel structure and utilizing the latest technology commensurate with a prestige rental office building. To achieve an exemplary building SOM undertook a major research program along with the design of the building. The main emphasis of this research was structural but it also encompassed other aspects, integration of lighting and air-conditioning, elevatoring (this led to the split core). Nine prototype structural schemes, all based on a column-free plan, were analyzed for cost, leading to the choice of the scheme built. The scheme selected uses the fireproofed flanges to protect the unfireproofed web, providing a significant saving in cladding. An additional cost advantage of the selected scheme is the 6'3" deep girders which give a 50% column connection allowing a major part of the wind stress to be taken by the exterior frame.

A special zoning resolution was adopted to permit consolidating the total allowable floor area on the larger block leaving the other block for a park. This park is a tree-filled plaza similar in design to the plaza around the building. The site slopes approximately 10' down from Broadway to Church Street. The plaza with large steps at each end for seating was established at a mid-point on this slope permitting the lobby entrances to be at the center of the building.

The building has a gross floor area of about 2,130,000 sq ft, including about 128,000 sq ft in the two stories below the plaza. From the first level below the plaza, connected with the lobby by escalator, pedestrian passages lead to subway stations and to the World Trade Center. This pedestrian connection is part of a comprehensive pedestrian circulation system in the new Special Greenwich Street Development district.

Spandrel section. The spandrel girders are 6'3" high providing a 50% column connection which is used for resting the wind load.

Tower, seen from the World Trade Center. ▷

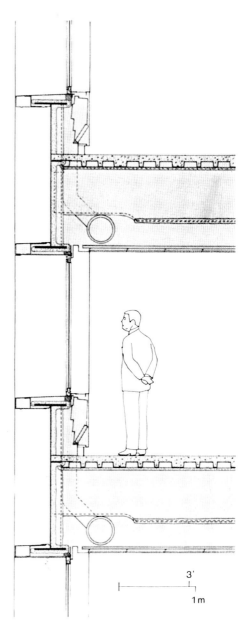

3'
1 m

Pages 134–135:
The first floor above street level is higher than the lobby floor and the typical floors.

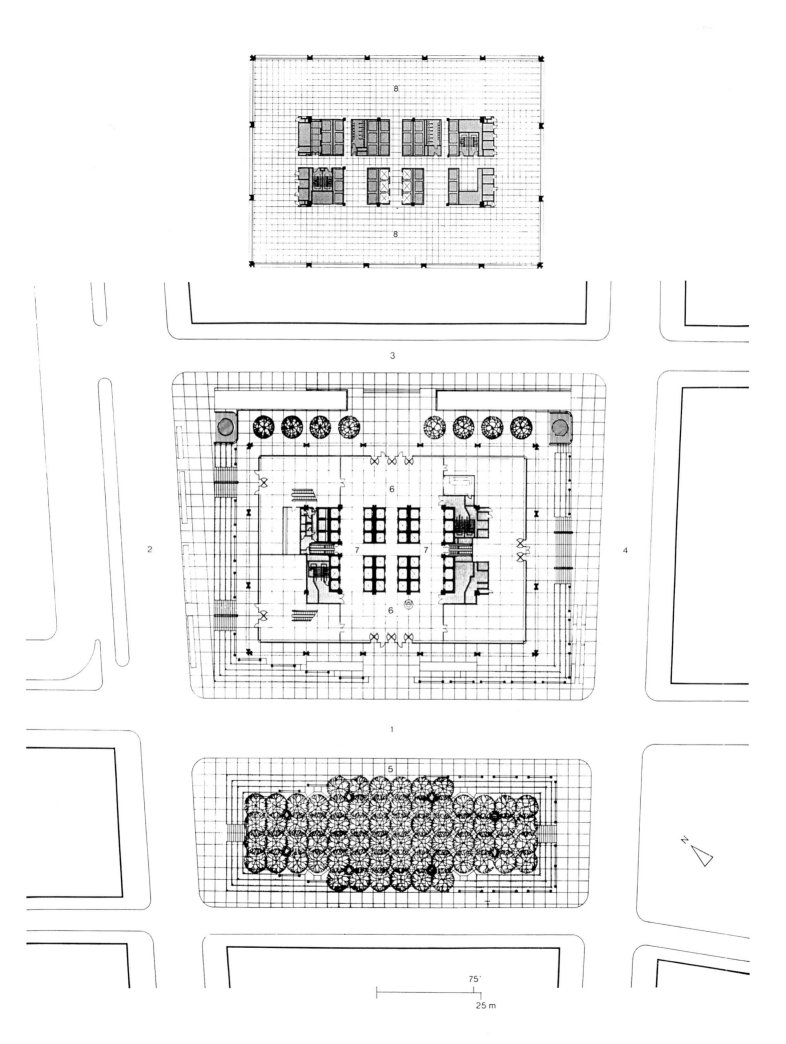

8

8

3

2 6 4

7 7

6

1

5

75′

25 m

Plans (ground floor, typical floor).
1 Liberty Street
2 Church Street
3 Cortlandt Street
4 Broadway
5 Plaza with trees
6 Lobby
7 Elevator lobby
8 Office area

South side of the building, seen across the plaza.

Southwest corner.

South elevation. Trinity Church in foreground.

View of the building across Broadway. In the ▷
foreground, the plaza of the Marine Midland
Building.

Alcoa Building, San Francisco, California

The building is set astride a three-level public garage designed by Wurster, Bernardi and Emmons and DeMars and Reay at the southern end of the Golden Gateway Center, a residential and commercial redevelopment in the vicinity of the waterfront. The floor area on the 24 typical office floors totals 400,000 sq ft.

The garage roof with the entrance lobby is two stories above street level and has become a handsomely landscaped plaza with a large fountain and four sunken gardens. Connection with street level is provided by four open flights of stairs and a set of escalators placed in a protected position next to the lobby.

The design of the steel framework was governed by the desire to find the most economical solution of preventing damage caused by seismic forces. The external members are placed 18″ outside the curtain wall facade.

The only members rising directly from the ground are the main columns which are spaced at 50′ while the intermediate columns and the diagonal bracing end above the entrance floor. As the concept did not fit into any of the categories listed in the Building Code, a computer analysis was carried out which disclosed a much greater strength than that postulated in the regulations although steel consumption was no higher than with a conventional structure.

The cladding of the external members of the structure and the framing of the curtain wall are of bronze anodized aluminum, the spandrels and glazing of similarly colored or tinted glass.

The building, constructed as an extremely stiff cage because of the risk of seismic forces, is set astride a public garage. The open space above the garage roof has been converted into an attractive plaza.

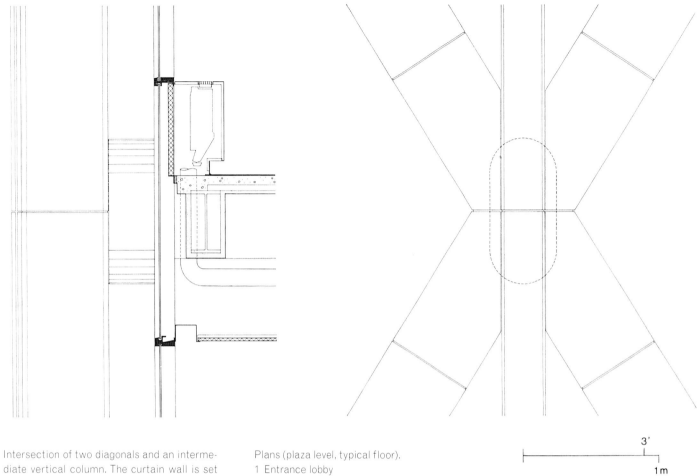

Intersection of two diagonals and an intermediate vertical column. The curtain wall is set
back 18″ behind the external bearing structure.

Plans (plaza level, typical floor).
1 Entrance lobby
2 Escalators
3 Open stairs
4 Fountain
5 Sunken garden
6 Restaurant
7 Office area

3'
1 m

N

60'
20 m

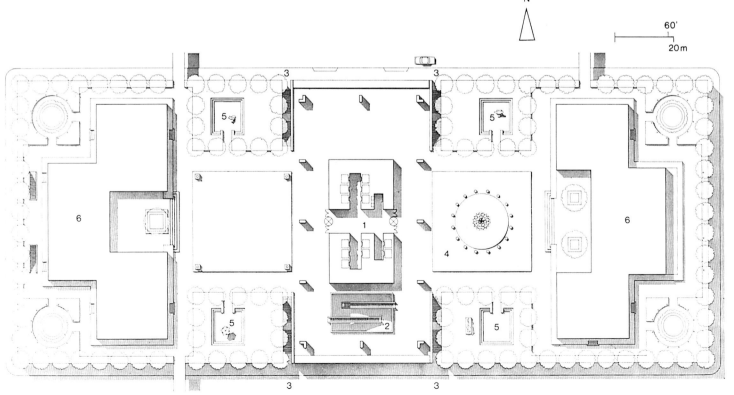

Corner office. In the background, right, is Telegraph Hill.

A view of the building from across the fountain. The claddings of the external bearing structure consist of bronze anodized aluminum; spandrels and glazing are of similarly colored or tinted glass.

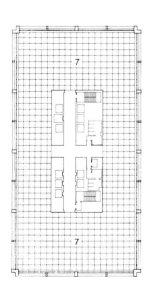

John Hancock Center, Chicago, Illinois

The John Hancock Center – known as "Big John" to the local population – is situated on North Michigan Avenue in a prestigious district with expensive apartments, shops, professional offices, hotels, restaurants, clubs and art galleries. The wish to continue this mixture – a pure office building initially contemplated was found to be unsuited if only because of the long distance from the nearest urban railways – gave rise, in the first planning phase, to the idea of using the site for a 70-story apartment tower and a 45-story, though equally high, office tower. But the two towers would have occupied most of the site and would have impaired each other's privacy and daylight conditions. Moreover, the apartments on the lower floors would have suffered from the noise nuisance of the street. It was therefore decided to construct a single tower where the offices would be on the lower floors and the apartments on the higher floors.

The tapered shape of the tower was chosen in order to match the different floor space requirements which decrease from bottom to top – from the entrance and commercial zones at the base and the parking floors above them to the clusters of small apartments at medium height and finally to the large apartments on top where relatively less space is needed for ancillary rooms with artificial lighting.

Structurally, the exterior members of the steel frame represent a tube where the necessary stiffness is provided by diagonal members and by those structural floors which coincide with the intersections of the diagonals and the corner columns. In keeping with the functional organization, this tubular body has its largest cross-section where the stresses caused by wind forces are greatest. Steel consumption, amounting to about 30 lbs per sq ft of floor space, was no greater than for a 45- to 50-story tower of conventional type.

Site plan.
1 Court
2 Mechanical installations
3 Car ramp to garages
4 Service ramp
5 Club

The tower is tapered from bottom to top ▷ in keeping with the functional requirements. Structurally, the exterior members of the steel frame represent a stiffened tube.

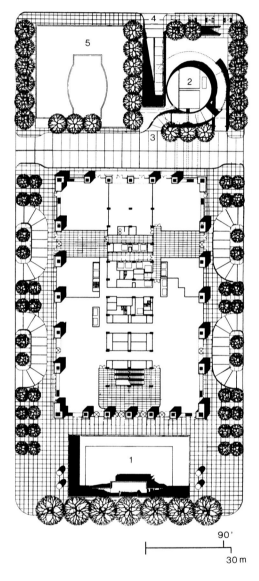

90'
30 m

Pages 146–147:
Rising to a height of about 1,100' (excluding the two television aerials), the tower occupies a dominant position on Chicago's skyline.

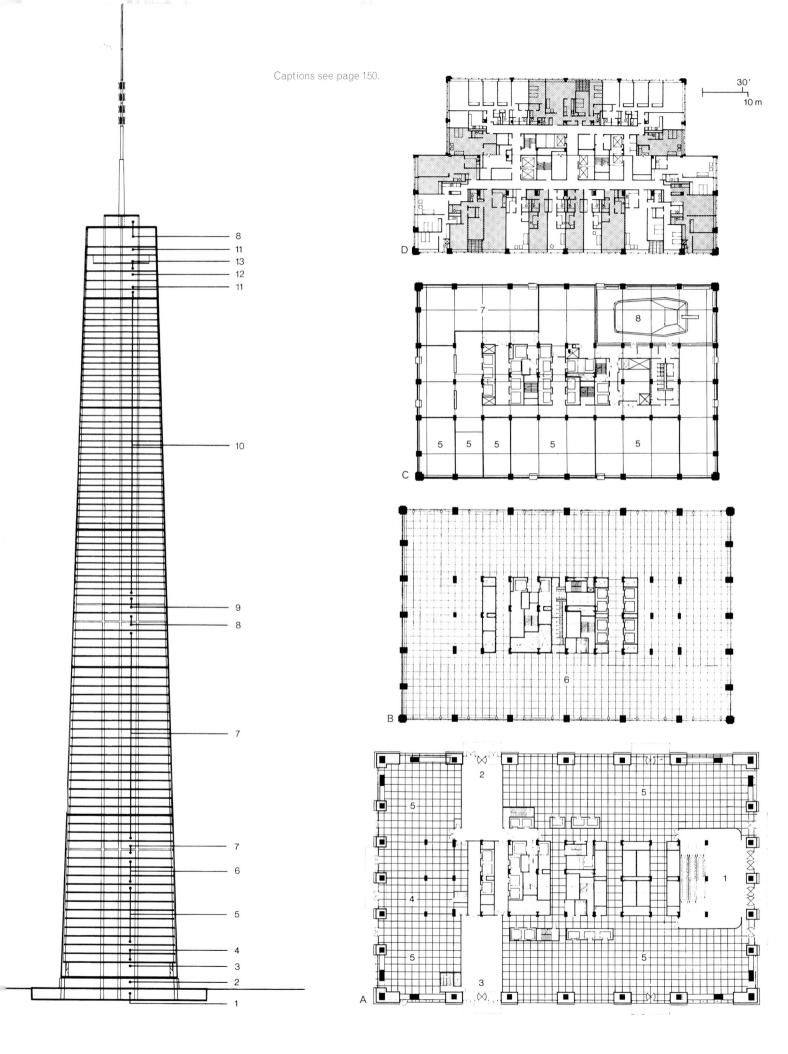

Captions see page 150.

Pages 148–149:
Section.
1 Commercial and service spaces
2 Main lobbies and commercial spaces
3 Office lobby and commercial spaces
4 Commercial spaces
5 Parking
6 Offices
7 Mechanical equipment and offices
8 Mechanical equipment
9 "Sky" lobby, swimming pool, restaurant and shops
10 Apartments
11 Television rooms
12 Observatory
13 Restaurant

Plans.
A Street level
B Typical office floor
C Transit floor
D Apartment floors
1 Office lobby
2 Restaurant lobby
3 Apartment lobby
4 Car lobby
5 Shops
6 Office area
7 Restaurant
8 Swimming pool

The entrance floor is clad with travertine.

Living room in one of the apartments. In designing the layout of the apartments, a point was made not to place small rooms near the diagonals.

Office lobby on the 2nd floor.

"Sky" lobby on the transit floor between offices ▷ and apartments.

150

Sears Tower, Chicago, Illinois. Under construction

The site on which the Sears Tower is being erected covers an area of about 129,000 sq ft in a rapidly developing business district at the western edge of the Loop. The gross floor area of the nearly 1,470' high tower – about 4,400,000 sq ft spread over four sub-surface levels and 109 stories – is the largest in any single building in the world, with the exception of the Pentagon. The owner is Sears, Roebuck and Co., the department stores combine whose offices are at present still spread over the entire Chicago area. Initially the owner will only use about 7,000 out of the 16,500 workplaces in the tower for their own requirements.

The space below plaza level will contain commercial areas, a cafeteria with 1,200 seats, service areas and – with direct access from the lower level of Wacker Drive on the west side of the block – a loading dock capable of handling 17 trucks at one time.

The tower is composed, in plan, of column-free squares of 75' side length. The first 49 floors which contain the owner's offices, requiring large floor areas, form a solid block of nine squares. Higher up, the tower is "stepped back" with two of the corner squares omitted from the 50th to the 66th floor, the two other corner squares from the 67th to the 90th floor, and a further three squares – leaving no more than two residual squares – from the 91st to the 109th floor. This design was primarily adopted because of the difficulty of renting floor areas of the great depth required by the owners themselves.

The squares are surrounded on all sides by columns spaced at 15' which take part in a cellular-tube frame. As it was not permissible to block the passages between the different units, it was decided not to stabilize them against horizontal forces by means of diagonal members as was done, for instance, in the case of the John Hancock Center. It was therefore necessary to use the more expensive method of rigid joints between columns and floor beams. The steel framework, preassembled in sections extending over several floors, has a cladding of black anodized aluminum and bronze tinted glass.

View from southeast of the "stepped-back" ▷ tower (model). The plan is composed of column-free squares of 75' side length. The first 49 stories form a solid block of nine squares; two corner squares are omitted from the 50th to the 66th floor, two further corner squares from the 67th to the 90th floor, and three more squares – leaving only two residual squares – from the 91st to the 109th floor. 152

◁ Views of the tower from different directions
(model).

Plans.
A Entrance level
B Mezzanine level
C 50th floor
D 67th floor
E 91st to 101st floor

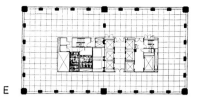

E

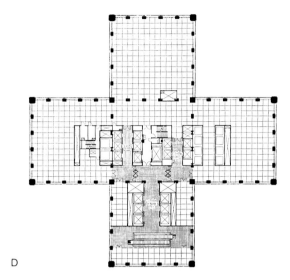

D

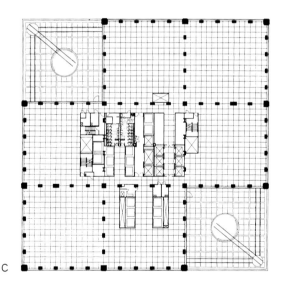

C

N

60'
20m

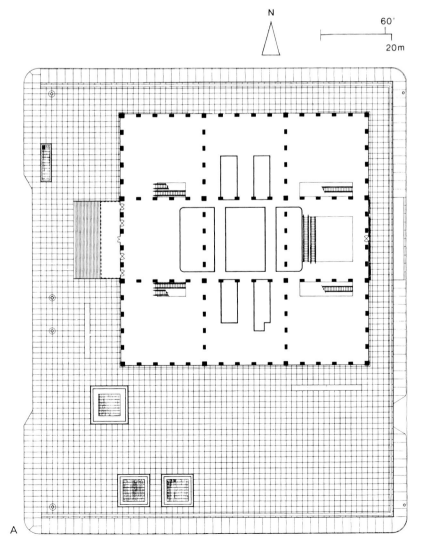

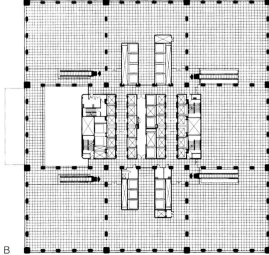

A

B

One Shell Plaza, Houston, Texas

With its fifty stories, this office tower is the tallest reinforced concrete building in the world. It is situated on a podium raised by 4' above the ground on a site facing the City Hall Park. The Shell Oil Company is the principal tenant.

On the three lowest levels are storage areas and parking facilities for 365 cars. The "Mall" level immediately below the podium contains shops, cafeteria, loading bays and a post office, and is connected by a tunnel to the existing network of downtown sub-surface shopping arcades. At podium level are the entrance lobbies on the long sides and exhibition areas on the short sides of the tower. The mezzanine level directly above the podium is taken up by banking facilities. On the following 42 floors are freely divisible office areas, averaging 20,000 sq ft each. On the three top floors are a club, a restaurant and an observation gallery.

The structural design of the tower is based on a "tube within a tube" concept. The outer tube is composed of a series of closely spaced columns and high spandrel beams. The increased depth of columns at eight points around the building provides supplementary wind stiffening while conveying the impression of undulated walls and giving indication of the unconventional system of statics. The inner tube is formed by the core shear walls enclosing building services and elevator shafts. With a maximum deflection from the vertical of 1/1,300th of its height, the tower has an extremely high stability. Even so, it was possible to construct it at the unit price of a conventional 35-story structure. The weight of the tower is spread by means of an about 8' thick, "floating" concrete pad. The need for expensive waterproofing was eliminated by the installation of a special draining system which keeps the water table permanently below the critical level.

The exterior of the building is sheathed in Italian travertine; the windows are glazed with bronze tinted glass; internal partitions are of gypsum.

The tower, seen from the City Hall Park. ▷
The structure is a "tube within a tube," with the outer tube composed of closely spaced columns and high spandrel beams. Deeper columns at eight points provide additional wind bracing for enhanced stability while conveying the impression of an undulating wall.

Banking facilities on mezzanine level.

Plans (podium level, typical floor).
1 Lobby
2 Exhibition area
3 Core
4 Office area

View, across the City Hall Park, of the north- ▷ west side of the building.

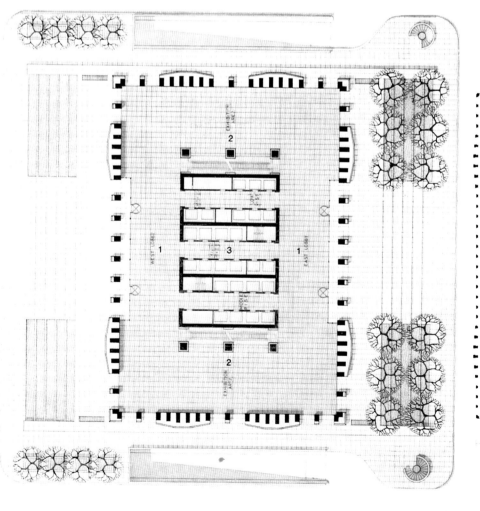

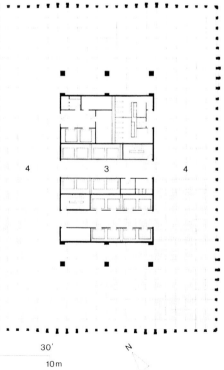

30'

10m

N

Albright Knox Art Gallery, Buffalo, New York

It was the intention in designing the new wing to enhance and preserve the appearance of the earlier neoclassic marble building designed by Edward B. Green in 1905. This has been achieved by containing all the new spaces – except the transparent glass cubes of auditorium and vestibule – within marble walls which extend from the base of the original building.

The center of the new wing is a large outdoor sculpture courtyard which is on axis with the entrance and enclosed by two exhibition galleries, an office wing and a cafeteria. On its south side, placed several steps lower than the courtyard, is a large exhibition gallery which can be partitioned at will by movable screens. Above the gallery is the auditorium which has a seating capacity of 350 people. The glass walls of the auditorium are of dark gray glass permitting the use of the projector even in daytime without having to draw the curtains.

The entrance to the museum was moved to the new wing so that it could be at ground level. The existing building and the new wing were connected where they overlapped by a large stairway ascending in a two-story well.

View of the museum at night, seen from north- ▷ west. The glass-encased auditorium and the new vestibule are the only parts to protrude beyond the marble walls of the new wing which extend the base of the original building.

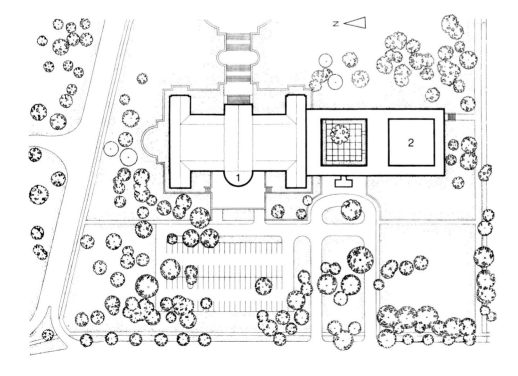

Site plan.
1 Original building
2 New wing

Plans of new wing (ground floor, upper ▷
floor).
  1 Vestibule
  2 Gallery
  3 Stairs to galleries in original building
  4 Cloakroom
  5 Offices
  6 Sculpture courtyard
  7 Dining room
  8 Kitchen
  9 Stairs to auditorium
10 Exhibition gallery
11 Auditorium

160

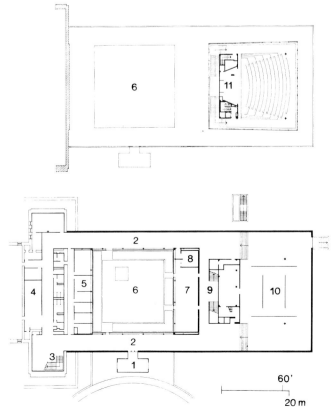

Pages 162–163:
View from southwest.

60'

20 m

Exhibition gallery on the entrance side, with the sculpture courtyard on the left.

The exhibition gallery below the auditorium is placed several steps below the level of the courtyard and can be partitioned at will. The grid pattern of the ceiling supplies air and electricity.

The auditorium has a capacity of 350 people. The dark gray glass walls permit the use of the projector even in daytime without the necessity of drawing the curtains.

The sculpture courtyard is flanked on one side by the auditorium and on the other side by the imposing columned facade of the older building so that an interesting contrast is created.

Joseph H. Hirshhorn Museum and Sculpture Garden, Washington, D. C.
Under construction

The building is to be a public museum under the administration of the Smithsonian Institution, serving as a permanent home for the collection of contemporary art assembled by Joseph H. Hirshhorn and presented to the American people.

The site made available by Congress crosses the Mall, the great linear park through central Washington terminated in the east by the Capitol and the west by the Lincoln Memorial to form a cross axis at the point where the mall widens with the National Archives. One important object of the architects was to avoid any interruption of the visual continuity of the central lawn of the Mall. Their solution was to place the massive cylinder with the enclosed exhibition galleries in a position behind the building line of the south side of the Mall with a sunken sculpture garden penetrating the tree border of the Mall and continuing the line of the cross axis.

The cylinder, covered in granite aggregate precast concrete and surrounded by a walled courtyard measuring 360' × 330', rests on four monumental supports which with their deep-cut sculptured ribs merge in a continuous flow with the exposed ceiling structure below the second floor. Apart from a balcony at third floor level which provides a view on to the sculpture garden and Mall, the upper floors are without fenestration on the outside. Colonnaded glass walls open to an eccentrically placed circular inner court.

The visitor enters the museum through the glass-enclosed lobby. From this lobby, escalators descend to the lower floor which contains gallery space for changing exhibits, an auditorium seating 280 people, as well as service rooms. Other escalators ascend to the galleries on the second and third floors. Access to the offices and research areas on the fourth floor is by elevator connecting also to the lower level service areas. Elevators and emergency stairs are within the four massive supports.

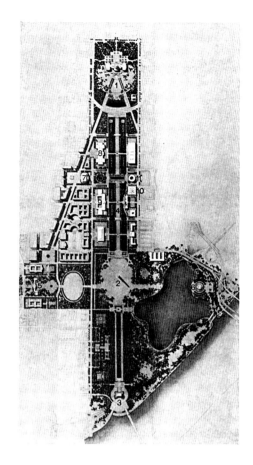

Plan of the Washington Mall.
 1 Capitol
 2 Washington Monument
 3 Lincoln Memorial
 4 Mall
 5 White House
 6 Jefferson Memorial
 7 National Archives
 8 National Gallery of Art
 9 Museum of Natural History
10 Smithsonian Institution
11 Joseph H. Hirshhorn Museum

Cross-section of the museum. In the center Jefferson Drive, on the left the sunken sculpture garden in the tree border of the Mall.

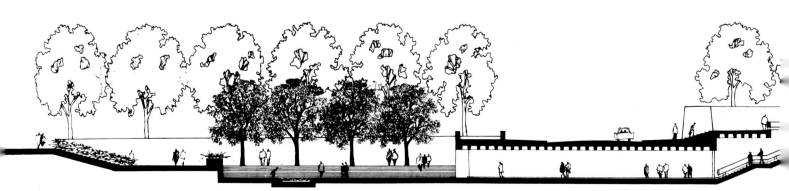

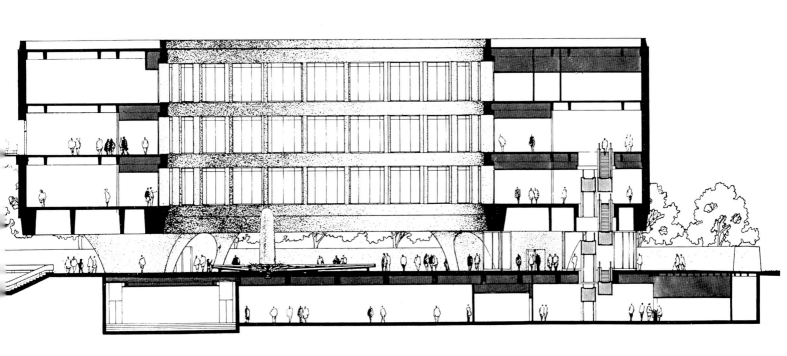

Sketch. The courtyard runs below the upper
floors of the museum, thus creating a large
coherent open space where large sculptures
can be placed.

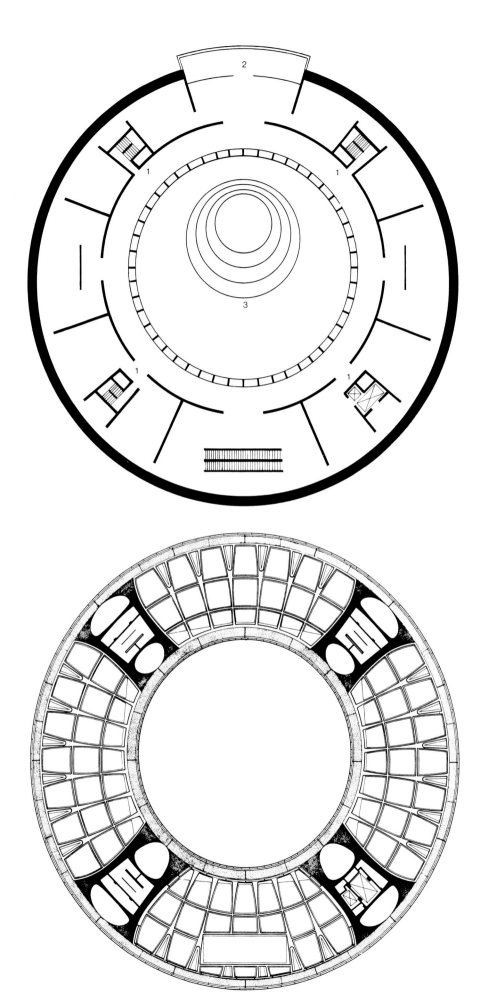

Plan (3rd floor).
1 Core with elevator and stairs
2 Viewing balcony
3 Central court

Underside of the exposed ceiling below the 2nd floor. The four monumental supports of the building merge in continuous flow with the deep-cut ribs of the ceiling.

Site plan. ▷
1 Jefferson Drive
2 Sculpture garden
3 Museum
4 Central court

170

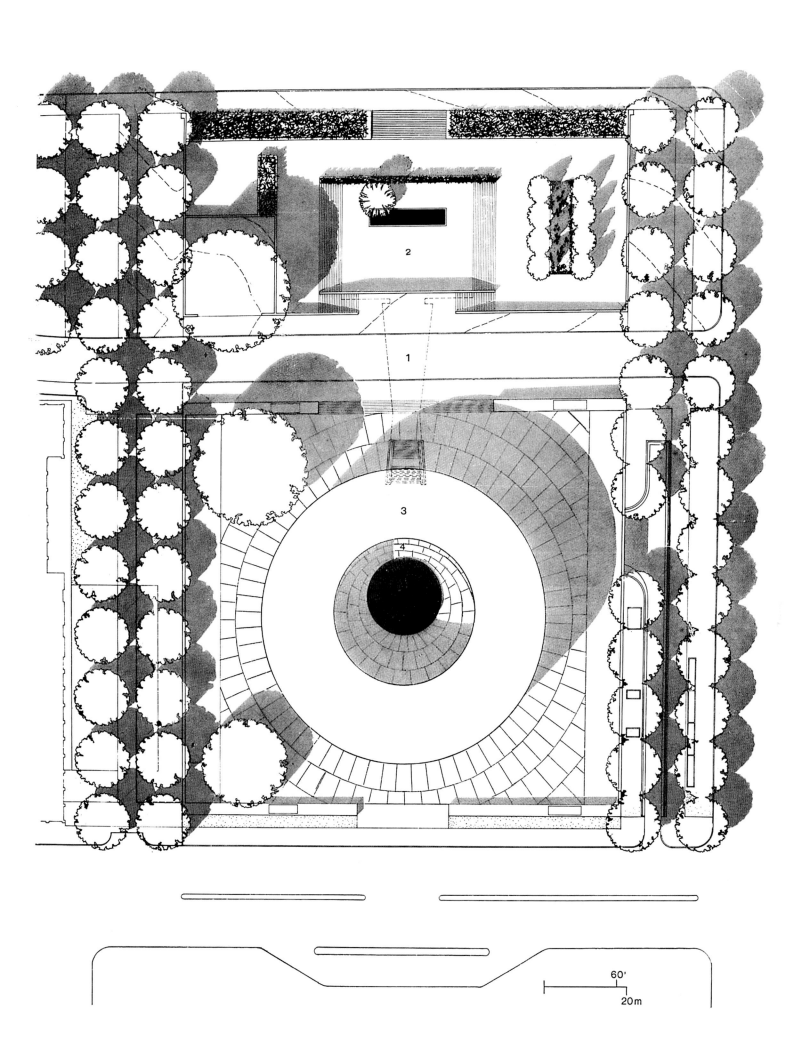

60'

20m

Beinecke Rare Book and Manuscript Library, Yale University, New Haven, Connecticut

All that can be seen from the outside of this library, which houses one of the most famous American collections of rare books and manuscripts, is a plaza and a large exhibition hall above an entrance lobby. All other spaces are placed below the plaza, light and too dry an atmosphere being deleterious to the preservation of books and manuscripts.

Below the plaza are two stories. The lower one contains mechanical equipment and a large book stack space, the upper one, an additional smaller stack space, catalog and reference room as well as a reading room and staff offices, around a sunken court designed by Isamu Noguchi. The entrance lobby at plaza level is glass-enclosed and upon entering reveals the vast exhibition hall. Wide twin flights of stairs connect both the floor below and the exhibition balcony above. In the center of the space of the exhibition hall are six stories of illuminated book stacks storing 180,000 volumes out of the total of 820,000 volumes and separated from the hall by glass walls.

The structural facade of the exhibition hall consists of Vierendeel trusses which transfer their loads to four massive corner columns. The trusses are 50' high, and respectively, 88' and 131' long and are composed of prefabricated, tapered steel crosses which are covered with gray granite on the outside and with precast granite aggregate concrete on the inside. Fitted into the bays between these crosses are 1 ¼" thick panels of white, translucent marble which filter the light and protect the precious books against the sun. The building is equipped with two independent air-conditioning systems, one for the book stacks and one for all the other rooms.

A view of the exhibition hall with the glass- ▷ encased, separately air-conditioned book stack. Illumination has been kept low to give full effect to the warm tones of the daylight filtering through the marble panels.

172

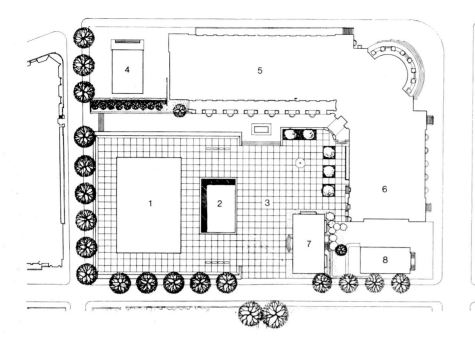

Site plan.
1 Exhibition hall of the library
2 Sunken court
3 Plaza
4 Book & Snake Society
5 University Dining Hall
6 Woolsey Hall
7 Woodbridge Hall
8 Scroll & Key Society

Plans and section.
A Court level
B Plaza level
C Exhibition balcony
1 Sunken court
2 Curators' offices
3 Reading room
4 Cataloging room
5 Catalog and reference books
6 Book stacks
7 Entrance lobby
8 Book stack
9 Exhibition balcony
10 Mechanical equipment

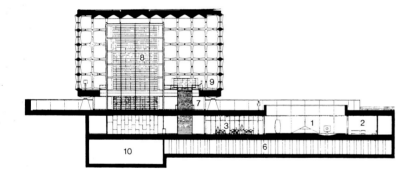

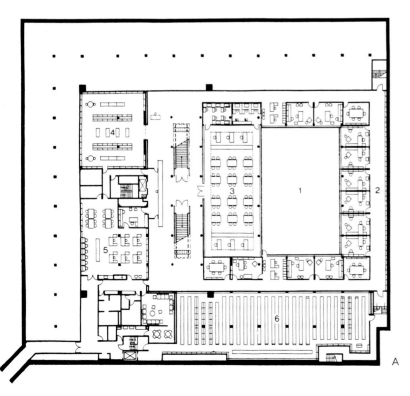

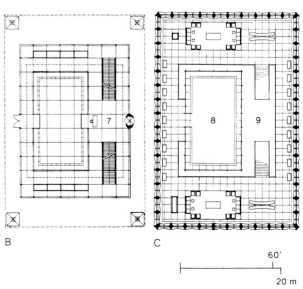

60'
20 m

174

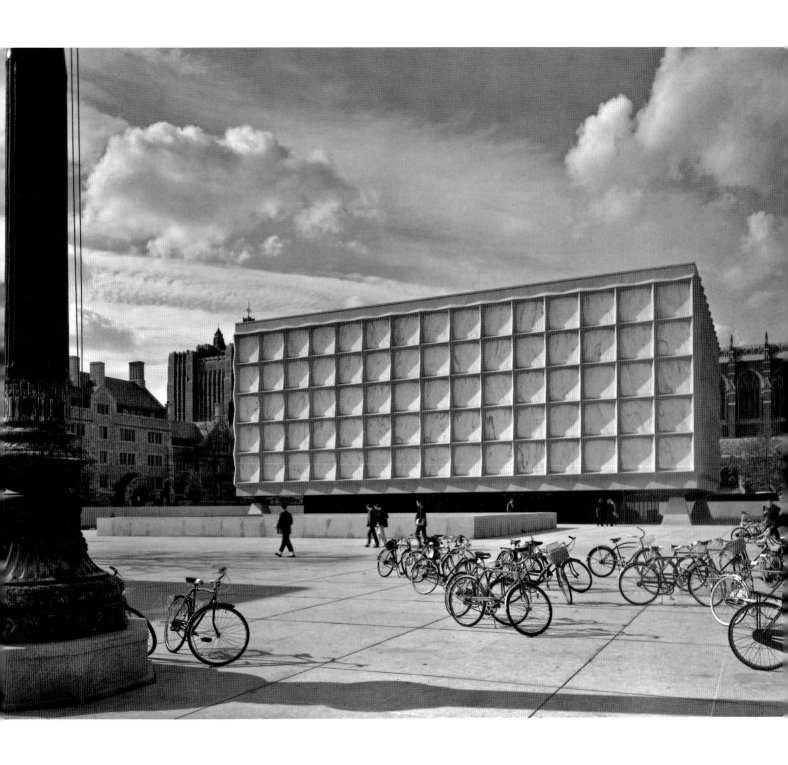

View of the entrance from Woolsey Hall. The low wall in the center surrounds the sunken court designed by Isamu Noguchi.

Pages 176–177:
Close-ups of the Vierendeel trusses. The steel crosses forming the external load-bearing structure are covered with gray granite on the outside. The panels consist of white, translucent marble.

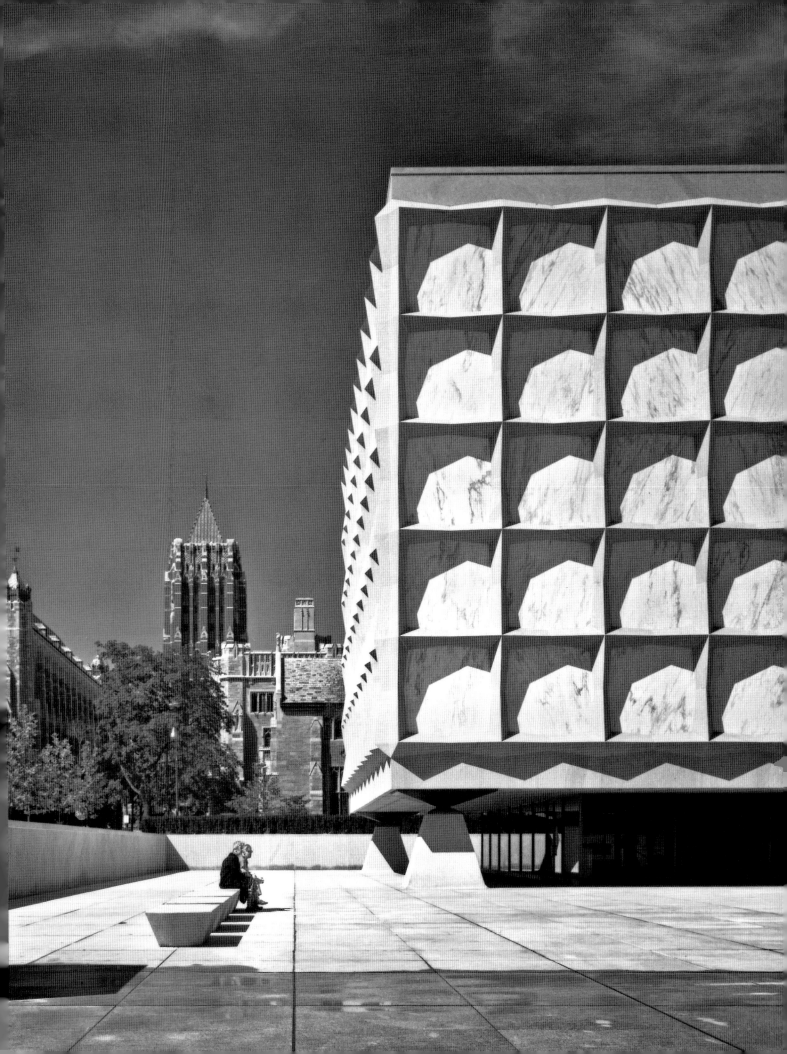

Lyndon Baines Johnson Library, University of Texas, Austin, Texas

The library contains documents and other material from President Johnson's entire political career as well as his term of office as President. Like the Sid W. Richardson Hall to the east of it (which houses the Latin American Collection Library, the Institute of Latin American Studies, the Eugene C. Barker Texas History Center Library, the Texas State Historical Society as well as the Lyndon Baines Johnson School of Public Affairs), the library has been designed by Skidmore, Owings & Merrill in joint association with Brooks, Barr, Graeber & White. The library is situated in the eastern part of the University of Texas campus which is separated from the central part by the small tree-studded valley of a river.

Two great parallel walls, some 200′ long, 65′ high and 90′ apart, define the main mass of the library. These walls, the end walls, the cantilevered top story, and the podium serving as the base of the building are faced in travertine. The tapering shape of the long walls delineates the shape of the columns which they conceal and which support the load of the top story. The ceiling box girders, together with thin connecting stiffeners, form a strong pattern visible from below and are supported by 3′ high steel pins separating the ceiling structure from the wall beneath. The space between girders and walls is of glass so as to provide a visual separation.

The main entrance to the library is at podium level. On this level is an exhibit area with displays relating to the official life of the President. From here, a monumental stairway ascends to the main exhibit hall extending through the whole length and width of the building with audio-visual displays and a small auditorium. The space between this floor and the ceiling girders is left completely free on the north side while the south side contains five floors filled with archives visible through glass walls. In the top story are study rooms, curators' offices, a small research room, reference library, and a suite occupied by the President in his retirement.

Site plan. ▷
1 Lyndon Baines Johnson Library
2 Sid W. Richardson Hall

Plan and section.
A Plaza level
B Main exhibit floor
C Top floor
 1 Podium
 2 Entrance lobby
 3 Exhibit area
 4 Main exhibit hall
 5 Auditorium
 6 Research room
 7 Interior court
 8 Reference library
 9 Curators' offices
10 President's suite

Pages 180–181:
General view of the library from the south. On the right, the Sid W. Richardson Hall.

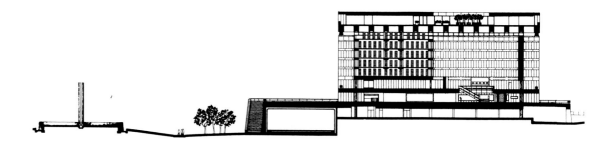

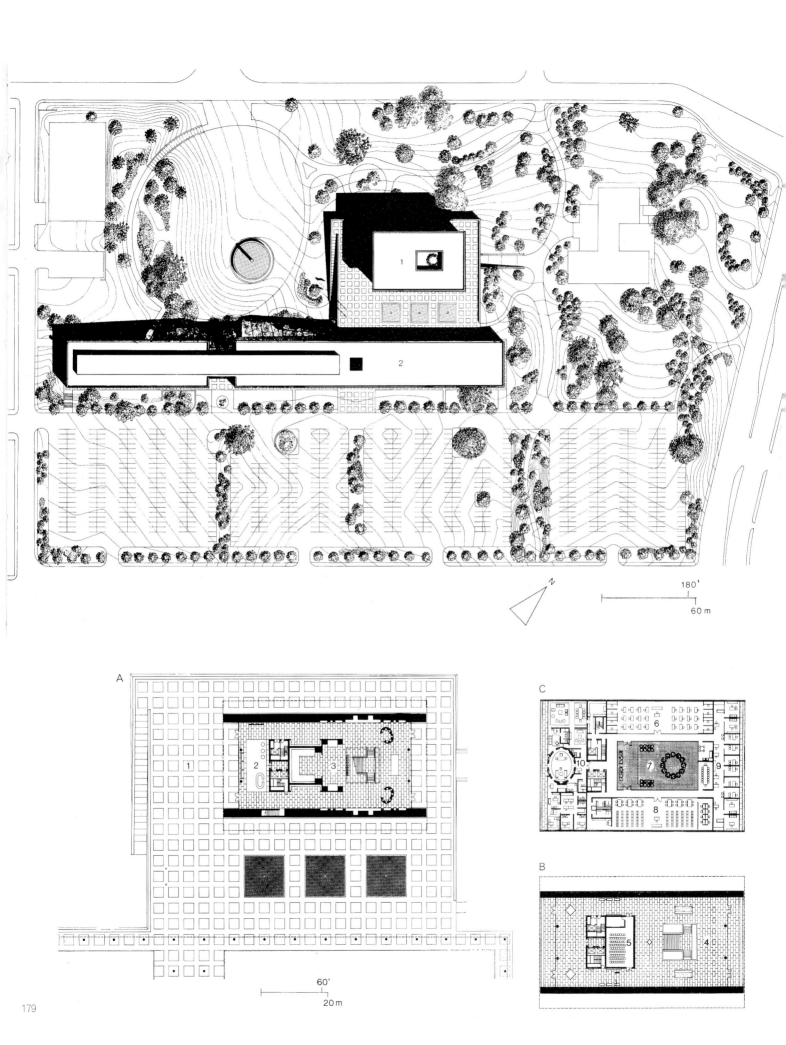

The tapering thickness of the two long walls delineates the shape of the columns within.

Because of their long span, the concrete girders carrying the top story were post-tensioned. The tensioning devices are of polished stainless steel.

The archives, seen from plaza level exhibit ▷ area. The documents are kept in red bound boxes placed like books on shelves.

Joseph Regenstein Library, University of Chicago, Chicago, Illinois

The library responds to the research requirements of the Social Science and Humanities Division, Business School, Graduate Library School, School of Education, Far Eastern and Asian Studies and the Department of Biology.

The program required that the book collection, readers, faculty studies and library staff related to each discipline should always be located on the same floor. This requirement called for the provision of seven floors, including two below ground, varying in size from 75,000 to 87,000 sq ft – a floor area about ten times as large as the average floor area of the other campus buildings. The resulting scale problem has, however, been overcome by an apparent reduction of the volume through judicious spacings and setbacks. Three primary constituent parts of the building are recognizable: a west wing with the book stacks, a central part with the reading rooms, and an east wing with the faculty studies. There are, however, no strict boundaries between these zones, as the central reading room zones are, where necessary, extended either westwards or eastwards. Moreover, the west and east wings are divided into separate units, with horizontal variation in the west wing and with horizontal as well as vertical variation in the east wing. The facade structures, too, are differentiated, with projecting and recessed parts forming strong contrasts in the vertical direction, the projecting parts being windowless in the wings and glazed in the central parts. The smaller windowless bays are taken up by carrels, locker rooms and service shafts, the larger ones by study rooms and staircases. Finally, a secondary differentiation is provided by story-to-story changes of a few inches in the depth of the projections. As the limestone panels of the exterior walls are in front of the floor slabs, the facades show a clear vertical emphasis which is further accentuated by vertical grooves cut into the stone panels.

Corner of the building. The windowless parts of the facades consist of grooved limestone panels.

South side of the central part of the building ▷ with the main entrances.

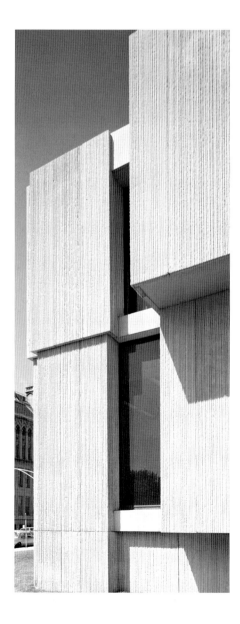

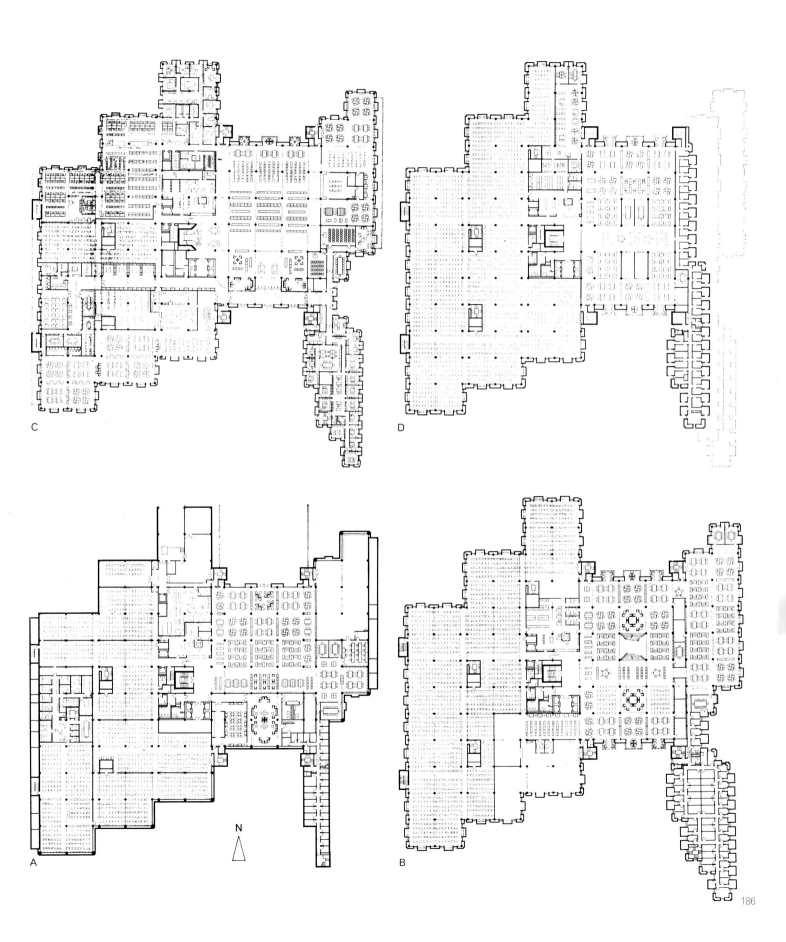

C

D

A

N

B

The library seen from southeast, with the faculty studies in the foreground, right.

◁ Plans.
A 1st basement
B Ground floor
C 2nd floor
D 4th floor
The highly differentiated building volume appears to consist of three parts, a west wing with the book stacks, a central part with the reading rooms, and an east wing with faculty studies; depending on requirements, the reading zone may be extended either westwards or eastwards.

Lounge at a bay window of the central part of the building.

Reading and rest area in the center of the central part of the building.

The 2nd and 3rd floors of the central part of the building are directly connected by a flight of stairs.

Louis Jefferson Long Library, Wells College, Aurora, New York

The library, covering an area of 55,000 sq ft, has stacking space for about 250,000 volumes, seating accommodation for nearly 350 readers, and a wide variety of group and seminar rooms. Standing on a slope, the building is planned on three levels, with one public entrance at ground level and another one at top level. These entrances are connected by a pedestrian street which runs right across the building and also serves as an exhibition space. To facilitate orientation, the layout of the shelves is different on each floor, following a radial pattern (except for a minor area in the north wing) at ground level and a grid pattern on the intermediate level, while the top level has a composite plan with a radial pattern at the ends and a grid pattern in the middle.

The layout pattern of the building is wholly, and the elevation partly, governed by the "field theory." The module is a square with a side length of 42'. Four of these squares, in staggered arrangement, form the core area, three separate squares each form one small wing, and two squares together one larger wing. The most dramatic architectural feature is no doubt the cedar wood roof which, with its multifaceted planes, matches the complicated layout pattern of the building. It is supported partly by isolated columns and partly by clusters of eight columns. These clusters, which also serve as wind bracing, stand above the centers of the nine basic squares and rest on strong masonry piers which are also used as air distribution ducts.

Consistent with the principle of the "field theory," some of the non-bearing plasterboard walls continue the slope of the faceted roof edges. They are painted either white – like the ceilings – or red or purple so that they form a meaningful contrast to the primary wood or brick materials and to the furnishings attuned to these structural materials.

Basic layout. Four basic squares form the core area, another five the four wings.

Seats and tables on the top floor, providing a ▷ lounge between the four central squares.

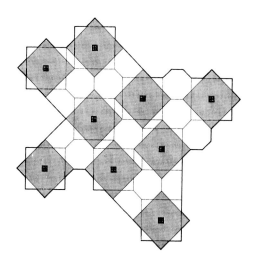

Library, seen from the northwest, with the lower public entrance in the center.

Site plan.
1 Lower public entrance
2 Upper public entrance
3 Staff entrance

Library, seen from northeast.

90'
30 m

Southwest side of the building, seen from the upper public entrance.

Plans (ground floor, 2nd floor, 3rd floor).
 1 Lower public entrance
 2 Group study
 3 Seminar room
 4 Lounge
 5 Newspapers
 6 Lending counter
 7 Catalog
 8 Reference library
 9 Administration
10 Staff entrance
11 Periodicals
12 Smoking and study room
13 Central lounge
14 Rare book room
15 Upper entrance

Lower public entrance. ▷

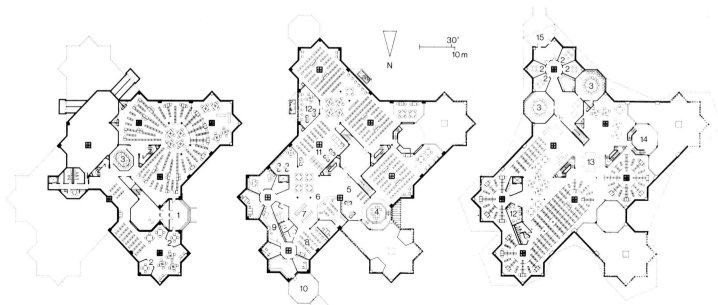

Radially orientated shelves on the ground floor.

Upper reading room. The wedge conceals the stairs leading from the upper public entrance to the lower floors. In the foreground, right, the easternmost of the internal stairs.

Lounge on the first floor. ▷

Social Sciences Building, Cornell University, Ithaca, New York

The Social Sciences Building at Cornell University provides space not only for social sciences studies and related research facilities, but also for psychology, sociology, economics and international studies departments. Faculty offices, student lounges and an auditorium for 400 people are included as well as the usual supporting secretarial and clerical service areas. The research facilities for the social sciences department are equipped with specially designed acoustical and environmental temperature control provisions.

Large, uninterrupted spaces free from structural supports have been provided to meet the program requirements. This resulted in the development of a steel structural frame which, as the design progressed, materialized in the choice of an exposed Vierendeel truss of weathering steel. A bronze heat-reducing glass and Border Pink granite aggregate in the precast concrete as well as a duranodic bronze finish on the aluminum window enframement were chosen as compatible materials with the weathering steel trusses. The structural steel framing for this building also serves as the curtain wall for the three stories from the second floor to the roof. Each facade of trusses rests on two supports 90′ apart and cantilevering 30′ beyond to the corners. Glass and window mullions frame into the flanges of the members of the truss to complete the curtain wall. The truss members are rectilinear and all members have an H-shaped cross-section.

The HVAC system is based on an all air reheat system. Outer wall and window heat losses are offset by hot water radiation.

The large, windowless podium on which the entire building rests is naturally used for the laboratories and auditorium, and the absence of windows aids the strict environmental controls required in these areas. Offices and other spaces for instruction are located on the upper floors utilizing the large glass areas.

A large plaza surrounds the ground floor of the building and provides an inviting space for students as well as faculty.

North side of the building. The site as well ▷ as program requirements dictated the use of a concrete podium supporting a four-story upper structure with a Vierendeel framework facade of weathering steel.

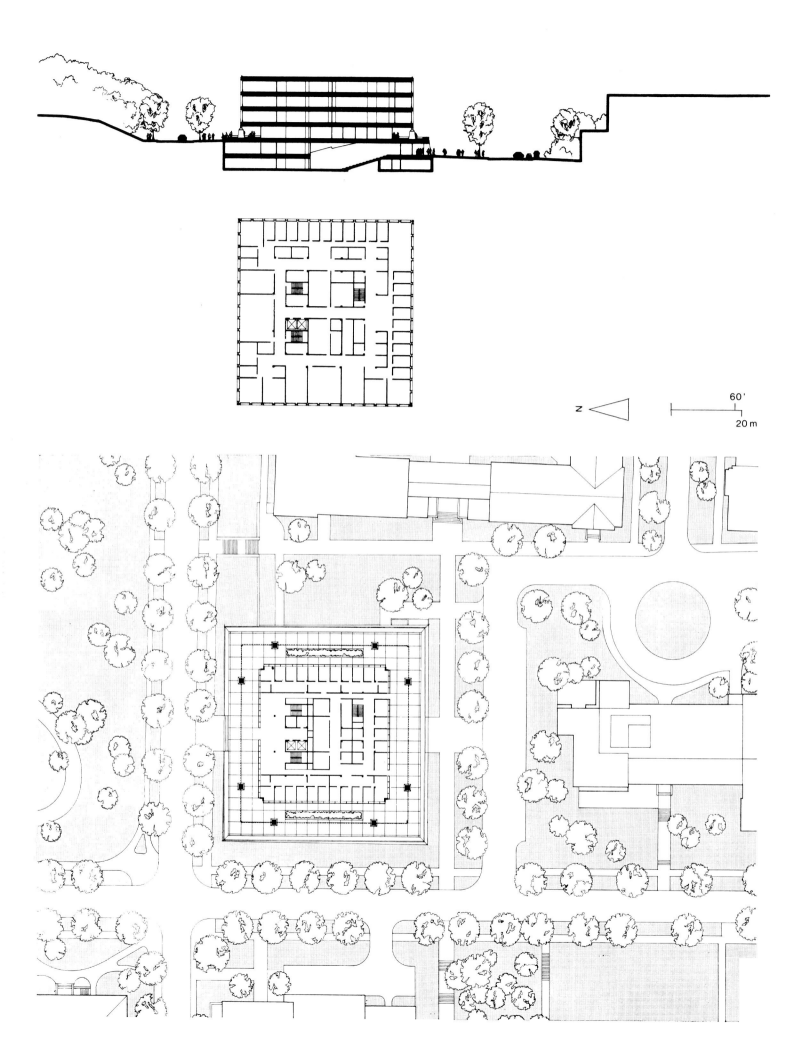

60'

20 m

North side of the building.

The entrance floor above the podium is surrounded by a plaza.

◁ Plans (podium floor, typical upper floor) and section. The auditorium on the south side has direct access from the street.

Annenberg Building, Mount Sinai Medical Center, New York, New York.
Under construction

The 27-story tower is the first stage of a long-range plan for the extension and renewal of the medical center. The total floor area is 1,047,000 sq ft, of which the medical school occupies 60 percent, and the remainder is occupied by central services for the hospital. There are no hospital beds in this building. The older structures which now contain beds will be replaced by future construction connected to the north side of the Annenberg Building.

In order to provide a site for the new tower, it was necessary to demolish several old buildings in the center of the site bounded by Madison Avenue on the east, Fifth Avenue on the west, 98th Street on the south and 101st Street on the north. The tower is connected at the subsurface levels and by several bridges to the remaining buildings. Eventually, the Guggenheim Pavilion on Fifth Avenue will also be demolished, thus creating a plaza facing Central Park.

Most of the ground floor is allocated to a 600-seat auditorium. To obtain column-free space for it, the structure of the 9th floor (which, like the top floor and the 3rd basement, is reserved for mechanical equipment) contains special trusses from which the floors below, including the roof of the auditorium, are suspended. All areas above the 9th floor are assigned to the medical school while most areas under the 9th floor are related to the hospital.

A 5' square module is the basic planning unit. Most of the vertical piping and ductwork is placed in triangular shafts integrated with the outer columns. The external cladding of shafts, columns and spandrels consists of weathering steel. All exterior glazing is bronze-tinted.

The ground floor is distinguished from the upper floors not only by its greater height but also by its travertine walls and its floors of brown paving brick, identical with the pavement outside. All the interior furnishings throughout the building were designed by Skidmore, Owings & Merrill.

Section of the building.
B3 Mechanical equipment
B2 Central sterile supply, pharmacy, medical records
B1 Outpatients department, emergency ward, radiology, cystoscopy
1 Lobby, auditorium, student lounge
2 Outpatients department, nuclear medicine, cardiopulmonary
3, 4 Outpatients department
5 Administration, faculty dining, public relations
6 Operating rooms, anesthesiology
7 Operating rooms, cardiopulmonary center, anesthesiology
8 Cardiopulmonary center, intensive care, anesthesiology
9 Mechanical equipment
10, 11 Library
12 Multi-discipline teaching laboratories, mail room
13 Multi-discipline teaching laboratories, bookstore
14 Neurology, pathology
15 Pathology
16 Microbiology
17 Pediatrics, orthopedics
18 Otolaryngology, anatomy
19 Biochemistry
20 Biochemistry, obstetrics and gynecology
21 Physiology
22 Ophthalmology, medicine
23 Medicine
24 Hematology, medicine
25 Surgery, animal institute
26 Animal institute
27 Mechanical equipment

View from the north. ▷

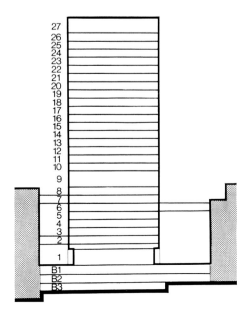

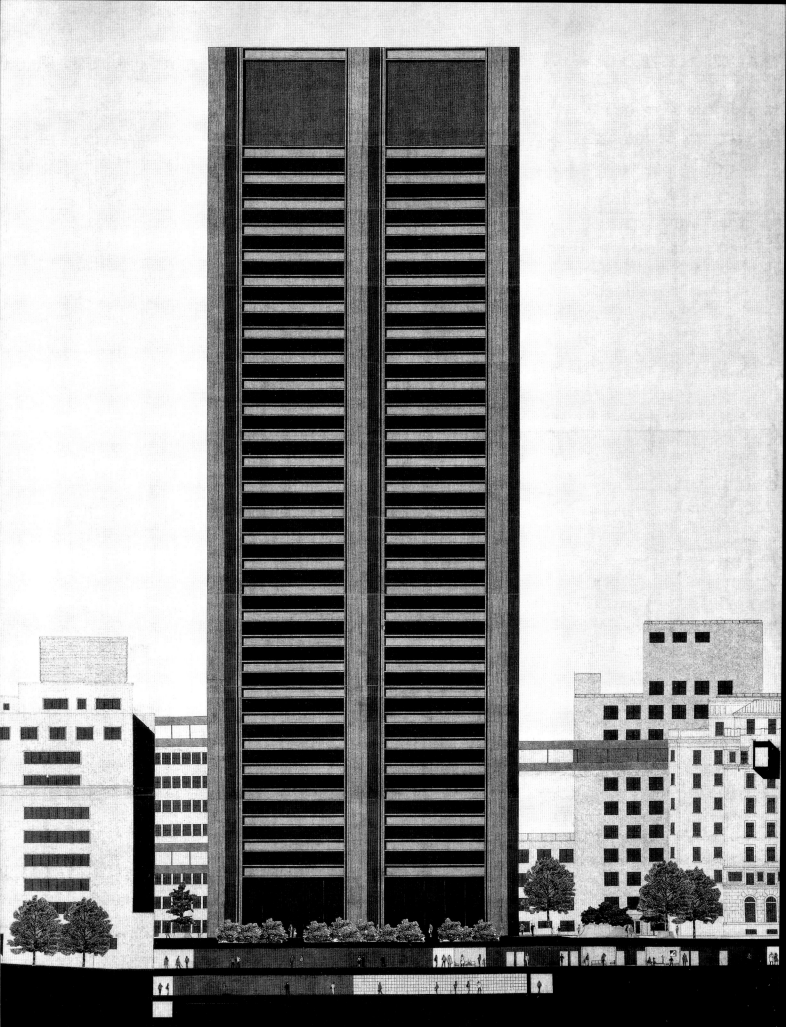

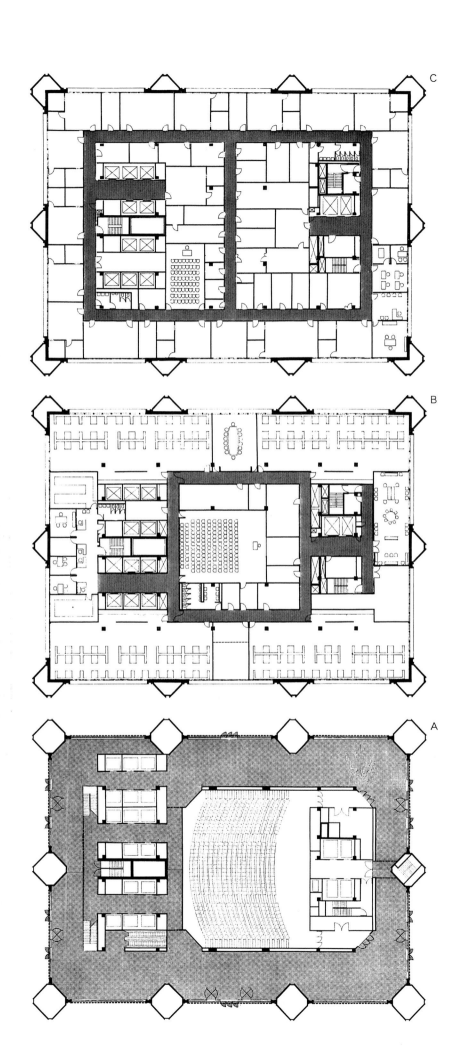

Plans.
A Ground floor
B 13th floor
C 19th floor
With its large plan area of 140′ × 200′, the building permits many variations in the layout.

View of the planned plaza (model). ▷

204

University of Illinois, Chicago Circle Campus, Chicago, Illinois

At the Chicago Circle directly adjacent to the Loop, three of Chicago's expressways converge, providing direct connections between the downtown area, the suburbs and outlying areas. Being located in the immediate vicinity of this important focal point and of a specially constructed rapid transit station, the new campus of the university, previously situated at the shore of Lake Michigan, is one of the most readily accessible sites in the city.

Instruction began in 1965 with 7,000 students; by 1975, this number will have been increased to 25,000. Apart from a very rapid progress of building activities, this enormous expansion rate has been made possible by the high degree of flexibility achieved, during the first phase and most of the second phase, by concentrating on buildings designed to serve specific functions – lectures, laboratory work, etc. – rather than specific disciplines. All the functions with mass movements of students were placed in low-rise buildings, all the others in high-rise buildings.

The first stage of construction comprised the following buildings: the Lecture Center, the first sections of the Central Library and the Science and Engineering Laboratories, the headquarters of the Students Union, the 28-story administration building as well as the central heating and refrigeration plants.

The second phase of construction, designed for an increase in the number of students from 9,000 to 14,000, comprised extensions of the Central Library and the Science and Engineering Laboratories as well as two new buildings, the initial phase of the Architecture and Art Laboratories and the 13-story administration building for the Science and Engineering Offices.

The third phase, just concluded, comprised the construction of the first mixed-use, interdisciplinary buildings – the Science and Engineering South Building, the Behavioral Sciences Building, and the Education and Communications Building. These new buildings are exclusively destined for the more advanced students in their respective fields of study while the undergraduates remain in the central academic area created during the first phase.

University campus, seen from the north. In the ▷ foreground, the 28-story tower of the University Administration, known as University Hall. All the buildings frequented by students are linked by a raised walkway system.

Site plan.
1 University Hall
2 Jefferson Hall
3 Grant Hall
4 Douglas Hall
5 Lincoln Hall
6 Chicago Circle Center (designed by C. F. Murphy and Associates)
7 Lecture Center
8 Central Library
9 Jane Addams' Hull House
10 Taft Hall
11 Burnham Hall
12 Addams Hall
13 Science and Engineering Laboratories
14 Utilities Building
15 Services Building (designed by Epstein and Company)
16 Roosevelt Road Building
17 Commonwealth Edison Substation
18 Raised walkway
19 Racine Avenue Building
20 Science and Engineering Offices
21 Stevenson Hall
22 Henry Hall
23 Plant Research Laboratories
24 Architecture and Art Laboratories
25 Behavioral Sciences Building
26 Science and Engineering South Building
27 Physical Education Building (designed by Harry M. Weese and Associates)
28 Education and Communications Building (designed by Harry M. Weese and Associates)
29 Rapid transit station

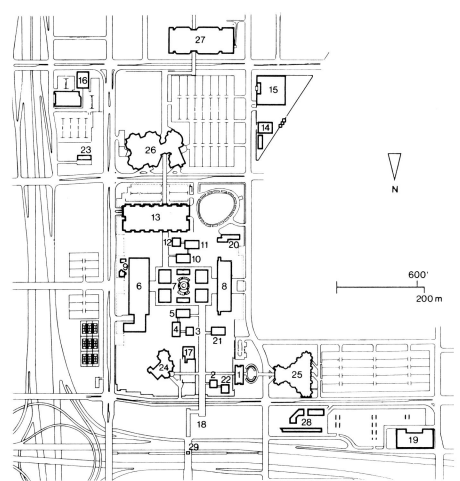

Architecture and Art Laboratories, University of Illinois, Chicago Circle Campus, Chicago, Illinois

The Architecture and Art Laboratories are among the first of a series of buildings designed on the basis of the "field theory." The basic unit of the structure is a square of about 80' side length, superimposed at an angle of 45° on a second square of about 85' side length. Each of these units is vertically offset about 3' from the adjoining ones. The units contain studio laboratories, workshops and a library. In the small intermediate spaces are stairs while the expanded octagonal spaces contain rooms for display, teaching, conference and storage purposes.

Initially, no more than three units have been built, providing accommodation for about 680 students. Another five units can be added in a second phase. After completion of the third and last phase, some 1,200 students can be accommodated.

As far as the layout is concerned, the building will not represent a fully functional entity before the second phase is completed. At that time, the unit at present containing the architectural department and the library will become a central core, surrounded by the other units forming a continuous spiral.

The bearing structure consists of reinforced concrete; the outer walls and most of the internal walls are of brick. To let the general design become apparent as clearly as possible, the outer walls are taken up in front of the structural floors (no more than a slight change in the brickwork indicates the floor levels) and contain only a few panoramic windows, shaped to match the geometry of the building.

The furnishings, developed by Dolores Miller & Associates, provide the students with variable workplaces in portable metal components.

Phase I building, seen from the west. In the ▷
foreground, the bridge connecting the Lecture
Center with the rapid transit station.   208

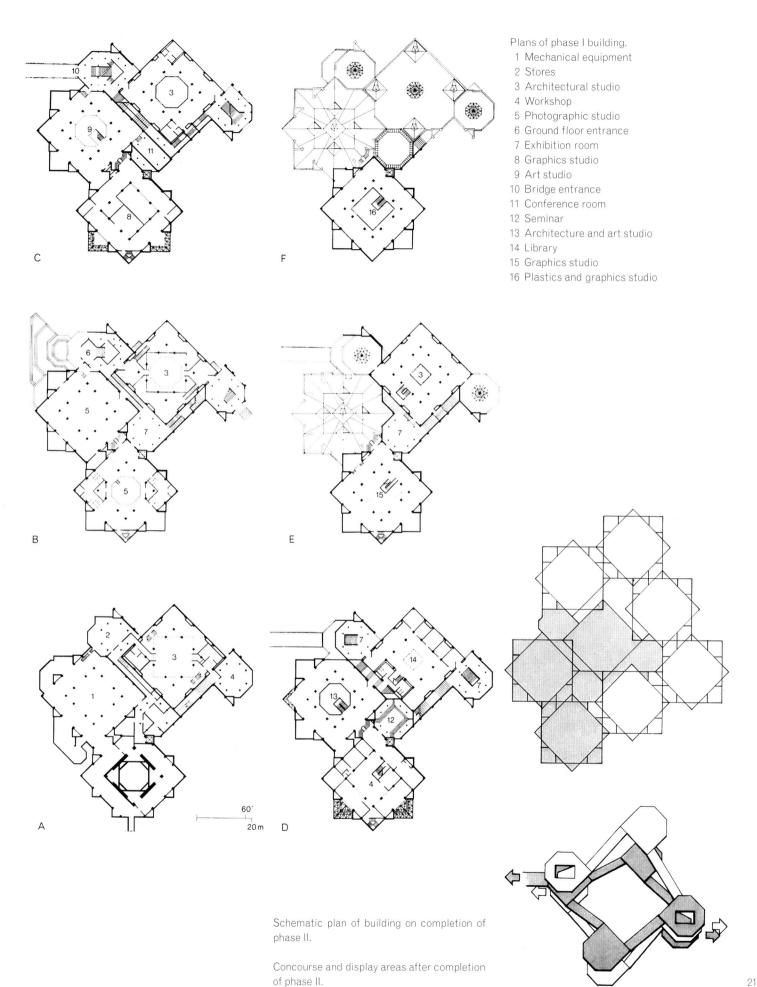

Plans of phase I building.
 1 Mechanical equipment
 2 Stores
 3 Architectural studio
 4 Workshop
 5 Photographic studio
 6 Ground floor entrance
 7 Exhibition room
 8 Graphics studio
 9 Art studio
10 Bridge entrance
11 Conference room
12 Seminar
13 Architecture and art studio
14 Library
15 Graphics studio
16 Plastics and graphics studio

C

F

B

E

A

60'

20 m

D

Schematic plan of building on completion of phase II.

Concourse and display areas after completion of phase II.

View of phase I building from the south.

Art studio, with the graphics studio in the background.

Architecture studio. The furnishing system developed by Dolores Miller & Associates enables the students to design their own workplaces.

One of the octagonal spaces outside the basic units is used as a seminar.

Behavioral Sciences Building, University of Illinois,
Chicago Circle Campus, Chicago, Illinois

The building contains offices and laboratories for the departments of sociology,
psychology, anthropology, geography and urban studies as well as a number of lecture
halls and a cafeteria with 700 seats, which are available for general university use.
Main access is via a pedestrian bridge, connected by a "traffic interchange" ramp to the
raised walkway system of the central campus.
The zones carrying the heaviest traffic – lecture halls and cafeteria – are located in the
eastern half of the building adjacent to the bridge. To distribute the traffic flows, the
bridgehead at the level above ground has direct entrances to the floors directly below
and above. The internal circulation space in the eastern zone has been designed as a
concourse for spontaneous congregations of students. The main stairway connecting
the lower floors is flanked by seats, used by students before and after the lectures.
The offices and laboratories in the western half of the building are screened from the
lecture halls by the elevator landing. Each office sector can be individually controlled
and arranged without impairing the general system. The offices are located along the
periphery and are clustered in star-shaped patterns around secretarial work areas inside.
The laboratories are in the center. They are mechanically serviced from a rooftop penthouse and suspended from twelve triangular shafts which are, at roof level, connected
to the penthouse in two separate groups.
Like the other two buildings of the University of Illinois described here, this building, too,
has a layout based on the "field theory." The structure is of poured-in-place concrete,
most of the walls are of brick.

The building, seen from University Hall. The areas most frequently used by the students are located in the eastern half, adjacent to the bridge connecting with the central campus. To disentangle the traffic flows, direct entrances lead from bridge level both to the cafeteria on the ground floor and to the lecture halls on the floor above bridge level.

South side of the western part of the building. On the left a stairwell which – unlike most of the outer walls which are of brick – is in concrete.

Plans (ground floor, 2nd floor, 3rd floor, 4th floor). The eastern half of the building contains a cafeteria and lecture rooms, the western half offices and laboratories.

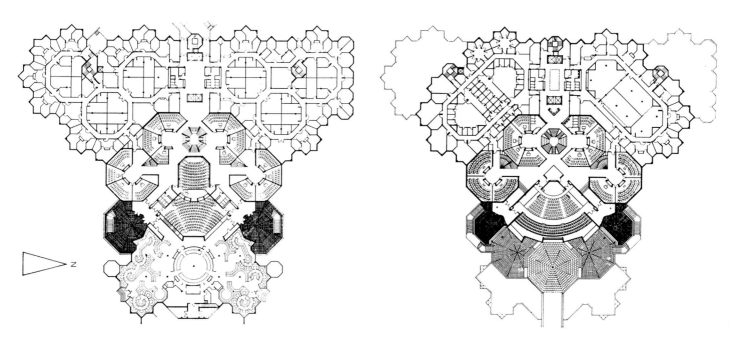

View of the building across the bridge. In the center the main lecture hall, flanked by terraces leading to the floor above.

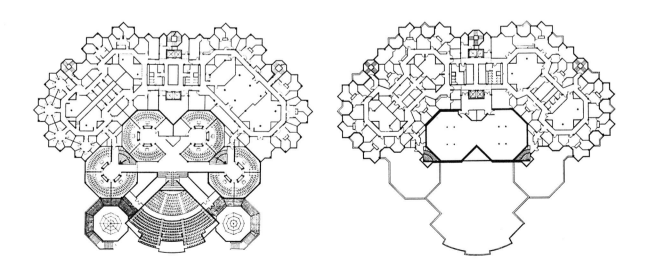

Science and Engineering South Building, University of Illinois,
Chicago Circle Campus, Chicago, Illinois

This complex represents the first phase of an extension to the Science and Engineering
Laboratories which are part of the original university campus.
The two parts are linked by a bridge which, in the new building, touches down in a
passage that widens out to form a kind of forum. To the east of this passage is the
laboratory zone, to the west the "public" zone, above it a library.
The five-story laboratory zone contains laboratories, workshops and offices for the
chemistry, biology, physics and geology sections. On the typical floors, four principal
distribution shafts form the centers of four clusters of laboratories, each consisting
of twelve module units; another eight shafts of smaller cross-section serve the offices
and ancillary laboratories along the outer walls. The four central clusters of laboratories
can be divided by removable partitions into rooms of different sizes. The partitions are
fitted with horizontal piping for hot, cold and chilled water, ordinary air, compressed air,
vacuum, nitrogen, natural gas and steam. Not only in the partitioning of the rooms but
also in the selection of fixtures, much emphasis has been laid on maximum flexibility. The
laboratory furniture, for instance, can be readily re-arranged at short notice, if desired.
In the public zone, one-half of the area is assigned to lecture rooms of different sizes, the
other to a cafeteria and bookstore.
The structural frame of the building – which is laid out in accordance with the "field
theory" – is of reinforced concrete, the non-bearing outer walls are of brick.

General view of the building from northwest.

Plans (ground floor, 2nd floor, 3rd floor). ▷
1 Passage
2 Bridge
3 Cafeteria
4 Lecture rooms
5 Bookstore
6 Library
7 Workshops
8 Laboratories and offices

218

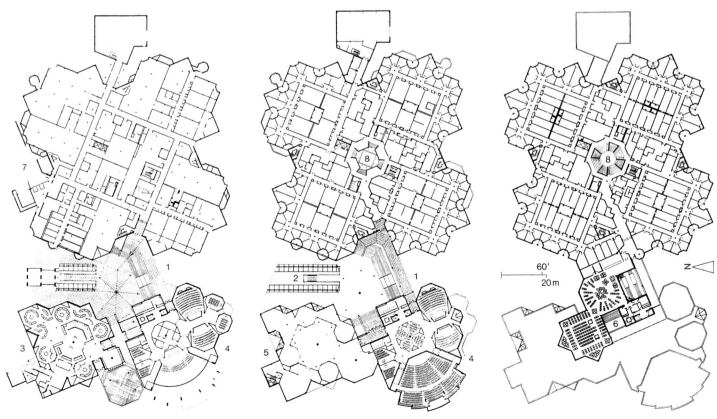

60'
20 m

Large lecture hall.

◁ Central stairs in the laboratory zone.

Laney College, Oakland, California

Laney College is the largest of several campuses simultaneously built for the six-city Peralta Junior College District. The site is located in a downtown redevelopment area in the immediate vicinity of the new Oakland Museum, designed by Kevin Roche and John Dinkeloo. Covering about 67 acres, the site is bisected by a channel which will be developed into a green-belt connection between Lake Merritt and the Oakland Estuary. The population resident in the surrounding district mainly belongs to the lower-income group which would not normally seek college-level training but may well be prompted by the immediate proximity of the college to make use of its facilities.

The college is designed for a total daytime enrollment of about 7,500 students and provides facilities not only for the usual academic subjects but also for a wide range of vocational subjects with special emphasis on inter-disciplinary contacts.

The building complex forms a compact group on an approximately square site. In the center is an open court, surrounded by library, students center, gymnasium and a base for a future theater. The outer corners of this cross are taken up by an outdoor work area, a combination dance and lecture hall, a physical training center and a nine-story tower for administrative and academic offices. In the outer zone are the teaching premises – with workshops on the ground floor and classrooms surrounding small patios on the upper floor – as well as a science forum and an outdoor swimming pool.

With its untreated concrete and brick facades, the complex has an appearance of strength and warmth.

View of the college from the west (model). In the center are the jointly used facilities, in the outer zone the classrooms and workshops. In the foreground the main entrance with direct access from a station of the new rapid transit railway (BART).

View from northwest of the nine-story tower ▷ containing the administrative offices.

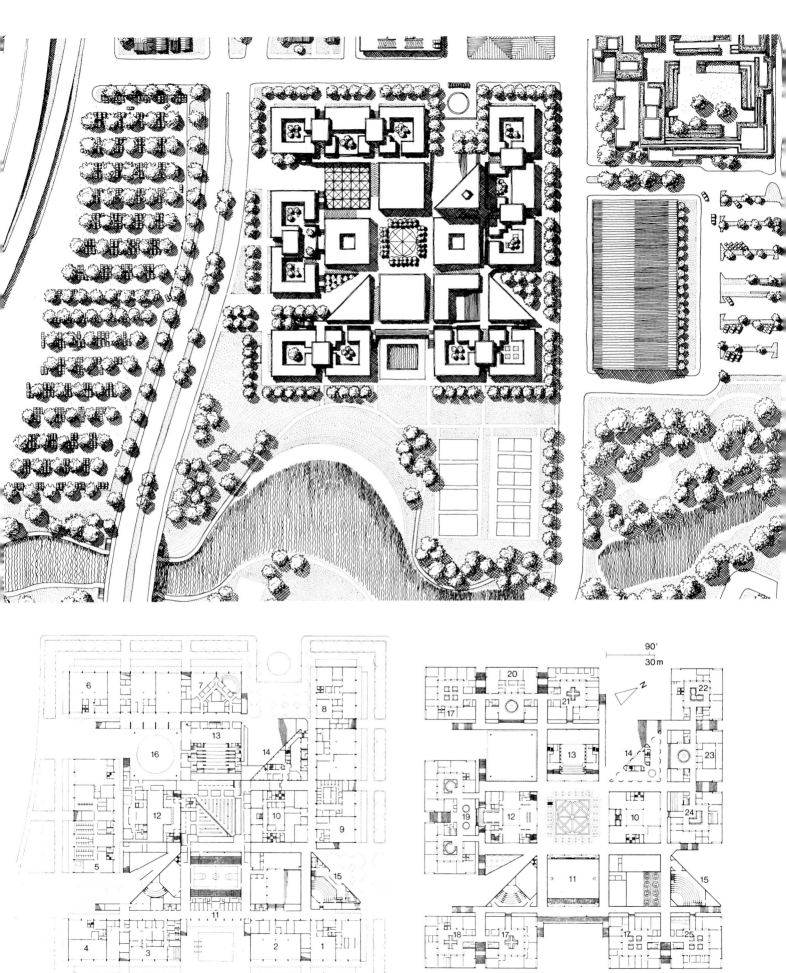

View of the library across the central court.

Theater under construction.

Robert R. McMath Solar Telescope, Kitt Peak National Observatory, Kitt Peak, Arizona

Named after its initiator who died in 1962, the telescope is primarily designed for studying the physical and chemical features of the sun. It is owned by the Association of Universities for Research in Astronomy.

The heliostat, weighing almost 50 tons, is placed on a concrete tower of about 100' height and circular cross-section. The tube is a shaft of about 500' length, inclined at an angle of 32° with the horizontal, and for the most part buried in the ground where the temperature fluctuates less than in the air. The upper end of the part emerging from the ground is supported by a steel jacket which surrounds the concrete tower but has its own separate foundation so that the heliostat is well protected against wind movements. Unwelcome thermal airflows in the open part of the shaft exposed to solar heat are counteracted by a cooling system mounted below the outer cladding. This system works with a liquid which will not freeze up even at extremely low winter temperatures. The jackets of the upper part of the shaft and of the concrete tower have square cross-sections, and their center lines are set at an angle of 45° to minimize the surface exposed to the wind.

Section of telescope.
1 Heliostat support tower
2 Heliostat
3 Optical tunnel
4 Mirror
5 Observation room
6 Spectrograph
7 Aluminisation room for the mirror

Close-up view. The square jackets of the upper ▷ part of the shaft and of the concrete tower are set at an angle of 45° to minimize the surface exposed to the wind.

Pages 228–229:
General view. From the distance, the telescope seems like a gigantic sculpture.

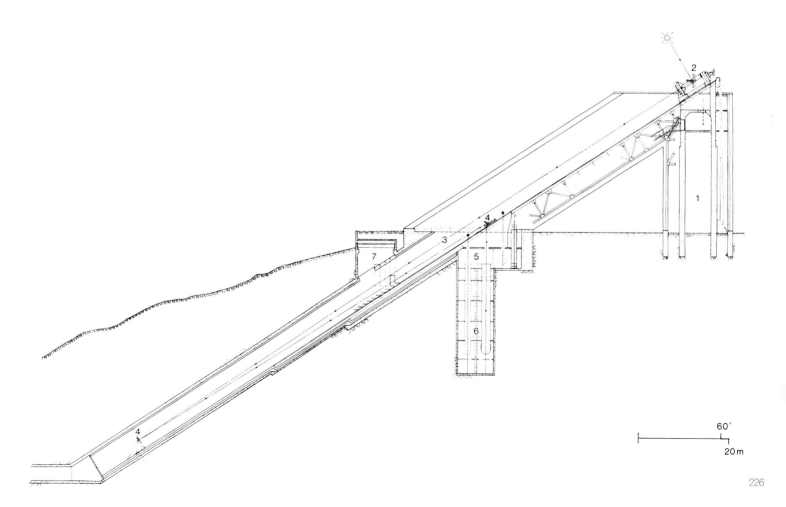

60'
20 m

Lindheimer Astronomical Research Center, Northwestern University, Evanston, Illinois

The building, erected on a tongue of filled land projecting into Lake Michigan, houses two reflector telescopes – one large instrument with a diameter of 40″ for research purposes, and a smaller one of 16″ diameter for teaching purposes.

One prime requirement was to protect the telescopes as effectively as possible against temperature changes, vibrations and wind movements. The designers solved this problem by completely separating the telescopes and their concrete piers from the enclosure.

The larger telescope is carried on a hollow pier of circular cross-section, the smaller instrument on one of square cross-section which also provides the access facilities – a small lift and a spiral flight of stairs cantilevered from the outer walls.

The steel pipe framework supporting the enclosure stands on its four bases with such a wide stance that it cannot be deformed even by very strong wind forces. The pipes are weld-assembled by means of circular steel discs or segments. The vertical parts of the enclosure consist of corrugated steel panels. The size of the units and position and size of the windows are adapted to a module of the corrugations – a detail which contributes greatly to the impression of machine-like perfection.

The lower floor, surrounding a small court, is partly below ground level so that it has the appearance of a base rather than a story. It contains workshops and service rooms. To reveal the structural independence of the enclosure, the lower end of the latter is placed so high above the top of the lower floor that it can be recognized even from a long distance.

The building, seen from across the lake. It ▷ contains two reflector telescopes – a larger one for research purposes, and a smaller one for teaching purposes.

Section. The two telescopes are supported on concrete piers. As a protection against temperature changes, vibrations and wind movements, the surrounding enclosure is a completely separate structure.

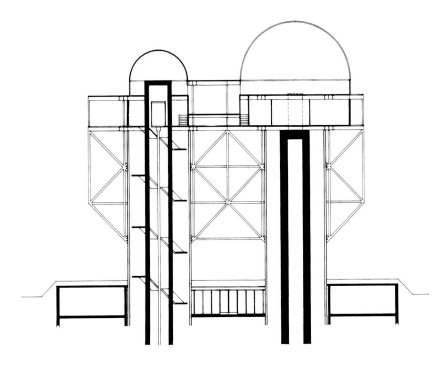

The framework supporting the enclosure stands on its four bases with such a wide stance that it cannot be deformed even by strong wind forces.

The two telescope rooms, seen from below. ▷
The pipes of the steel framework are welded together with circular steel discs or segments.

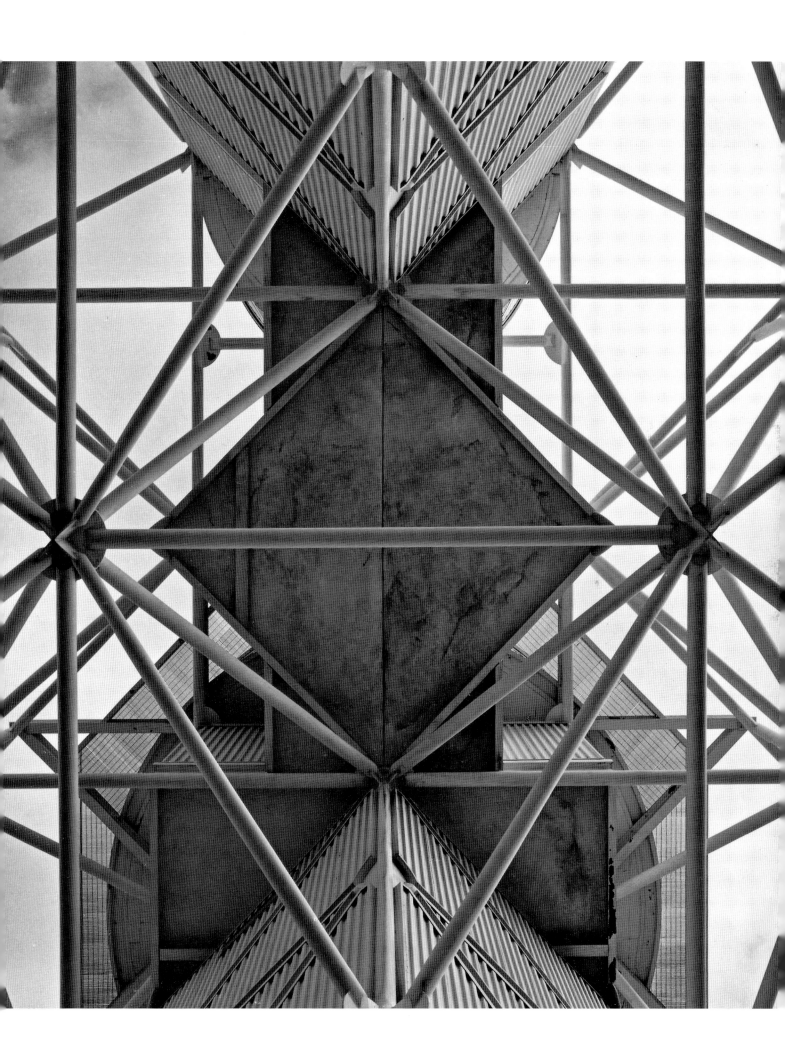

Oakland-Alameda County Coliseum, Oakland, California

Favorably situated alongside a major inter-city freeway near the population center of the Bay Region, this complex – designed for a whole range of sports and recreation facilities – consists of a stadium, an enclosed multi-purpose arena and an intermediate exhibition hall, flanked by two outdoor exhibition areas.

The circular stadium, with a maximum seating capacity for 53,000 spectators and an outside diameter of 770', is primarily designed for baseball, football and soccer. To facilitate access to the seats, the playing field was lowered 29' below ground level. The lower rows of the grandstands make use of the slopes of the excavated bowl, forming a ring around the entire playing field, while the upper rows are supported by a reinforced concrete structure extending around two-thirds of the playing field. Access to the upper grandstand is from the roof of the exhibition hall and a ring-shaped earth berm connecting with it. For football and soccer matches, a removable grandstand of tubular steel is erected in the eastern part of the playing field, and the pitch runs from north to south while baseball is played from east to west.

The exhibition hall has a floor space of 50,000 sq ft. By combining it with the immediately adjacent multi-purpose arena, a contiguous indoor exhibition area of about 110,000 sq ft can be obtained.

Like the stadium, the multi-purpose arena is circular in plan. It has an outer diameter of 420' and seating accommodation for up to 15,000 spectators. Of particular interest is the design of the roof which spans the entire space without intermediate columns. A ring of diagonally intersecting columns of reinforced concrete, which also take up lateral forces, supports an external ring of compression members, likewise consisting of reinforced concrete. Suspended from this compression ring are 96 galvanized steel cables, linked to a steel tension ring in the center. These cables support a system of slender precast concrete ribs carrying the roof, as well as a steel-framed penthouse 260' in diameter. Because of the inverted shape of the roof, the rain water is collected at the outer wall of the penthouse from which it is pumped up to the gutters along the compression ring.

Aerial photograph of the Coliseum complex, ▷ with the stadium in the foreground, the exhibition hall in the center, and the multi-purpose arena in the background. For football and soccer matches, a grandstand of tubular steel is erected in the eastern part of the playing field.   234

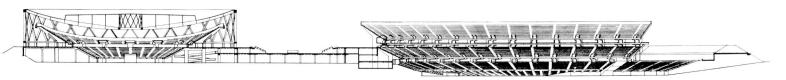

Section of stadium, exhibition hall and multi-purpose arena.

Details of the arena roof. Top: system plan. Bottom: plan of two bays, and sections of the outer compression ring (A), two longitudinal ribs with steel cable insertions (B), and the inner tension ring (C).

Site plan of the complex, with the stadium ▷ arranged for baseball.

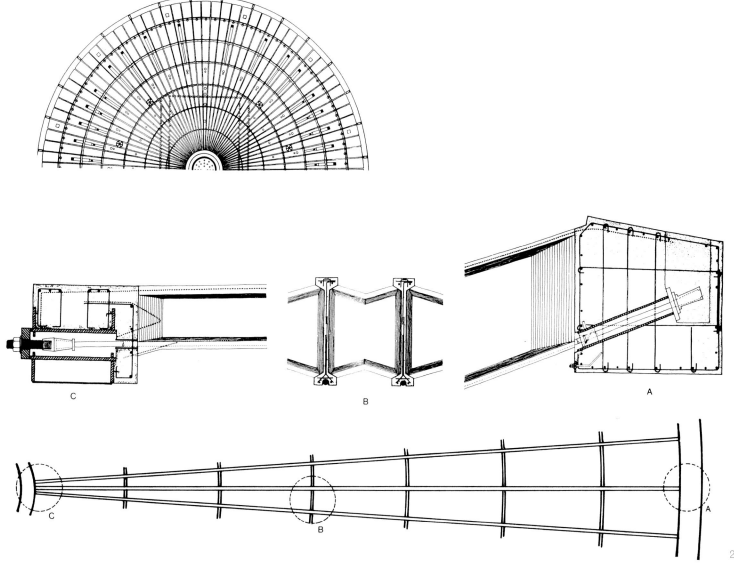

C

B

A

C

B

A

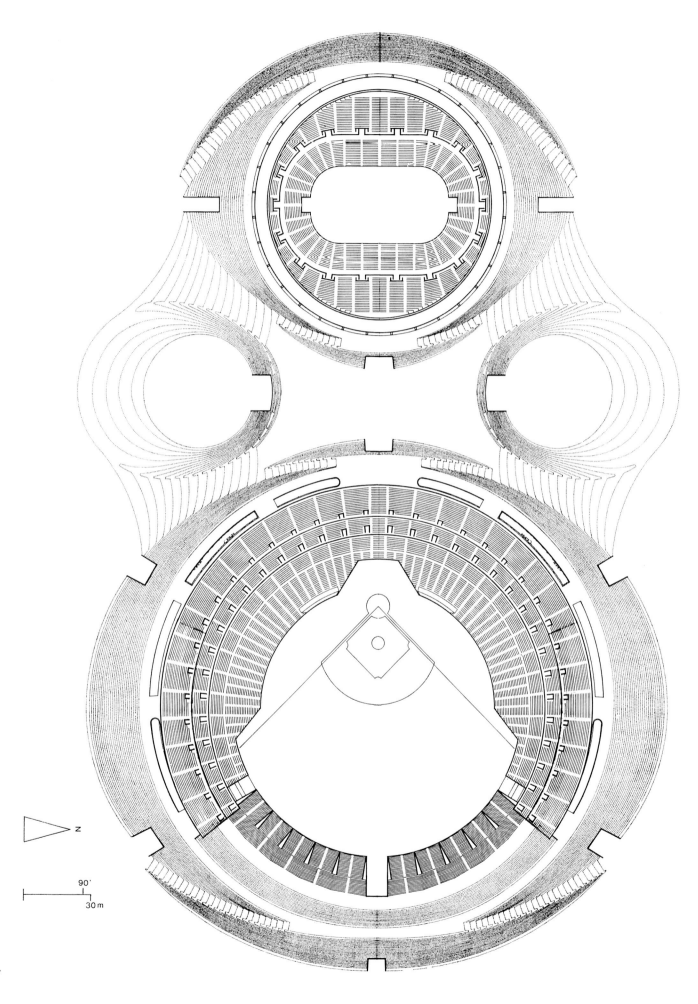

View of the complex from the north.

Nighttime view of the multi-purpose arena. ▷

Interior of the multi-purpose arena.

Ramps for the grandstands of the stadium.

◁ Outer concourse of the arena. The upper glass
241 wall is braced by trusses.

Housing Units at the Winnebago Children's Home, Neillsville, Wisconsin

The home, designed for emotionally disturbed children from seven to eighteen years of age, stands in particularly attractive grounds which cover an area of 180 acres on the bank of the Black River. The four new houses have been built to replace obsolete dormitory facilities. In addition, there are a large administration and dormitory building, a school, and two older housing units.

Within the grounds, the children have complete freedom. Their daily routine is much the same as in a normal family. They go to school in the morning – either to public school in Neillsville if possible, or to the special school on the grounds; they come home for lunch and return to school in the afternoon. The therapy mainly takes the form of informal, spontaneous communication.

In keeping with this pedagogical and therapeutical principle, the four new houses, each of them accommodating ten children and their house parents, are organized like large family houses. The individual rooms – four double rooms and two single rooms – are placed in ascending helical configuration around a continually rising common space where the children, supervised by the house parents, can follow their daytime routine – reading and study, hobbies and crafts. The exterior covered areas beneath the higher rooms along the periphery are used as terraces for outdoor meals and play and for the storage of bicycles, toboggans and other outdoor accessories.

Despite their emotionally stimulating spatial complexity, the houses are composed of individually simple elements. Each of the rooms on the periphery is a square box with a diagonally oriented gable roof. The common room in the middle is covered by four roof elements which are supported by three circular columns in the center and by the inner walls of the peripheral rooms. Bearing structure and cladding of the houses are of wood.

Perspective plan of a house. In the middle the common room, on the outside the bedrooms.

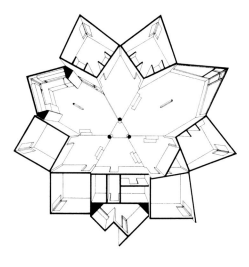

Entrance sides of two of the houses. On the
right of each house, the outdoor stairs leading
to the upper end of the common room.

Plans (lower level, upper level).

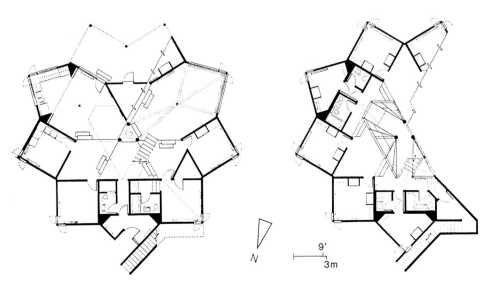

N   9'
                    3m

The common room ascends helically in keeping with the bedrooms on the outside.

Stairs leading to the upper end of the common room.

Common room. In the background, left, the circular columns in the center of the house.

Two houses, seen from across the river.

Carmel Valley Manor, Carmel Valley, California

This village for the elderly is situated 7 miles outside Carmel, a small coastal town southwest of Monterey, which has given its name to the isolated, very attractive valley in the Santa Lucia Range. Covering 26 acres, the site begins on the south side with a low meadow along the valley road and rises fairly rapidly towards the center before swinging gently towards the foothills on the right-hand side of the valley.

The general facilities for the village are located in the center of the site. The cruciform main building contains the administrative offices, a lounge, a dining room, an infirmary as well as craft rooms. In the two ancillary buildings are smaller lounges, reading rooms and laundry facilities. The chapel is designed so that it can also be used for other social activities.

Among the 170 residential units are 48 units for single persons without cooking facilities (but with sink and refrigerator), 72 two-room units with kitchenette, 32 three-room units with separate kitchen and 18 three-room units with separate kitchen and additional bathroom. The single-room units are located in three two-story buildings, connected to the main building by covered walks, the two-room units in nine single-story buildings, the smaller three-room units in eight single-story buildings with open courts, and the larger three-room units in nine pairs of cottages separated by carports.

Except for the chapel which has a wooden roof supported by steel trusses, and the two-story town houses where regulations called for steel frames, all buildings have timber frames. The walls have a cladding of gypsumboard on the inside and white stucco coating on the outside. The roofing consists of redwood shingles.

The architectural design was clearly influenced by traditional Californian styles and their Mediterranean, especially Spanish, forerunners. One of the reasons for this choice was the original requirement to integrate with the new complex a colonial-style house dating back to the 1920s which was, however, destroyed by fire during the planning stage.

General view of the retirement village from
the north.

Site plan.
1 Main road
2 Main building
3 Ancillary buildings
4 Chapel
5 Two-story house with 16 single-room units
6 Single-story house with eight two-room
   units
7 Single-story house with four smaller three-
   room units
8 Single-story house with two larger three-
   room units separated by carports
9 Carports
10 Swimming pool

150'
50 m

One of the single-story houses with two-room units.

Court of one of the single-story houses with smaller three-room units.

Plans of the different types of residential ▷ units.
A Single-room unit
B Two-room unit
C Three-room unit with one bathroom
D Three-room unit with two bathrooms and carport

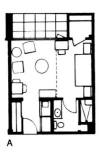

A

B

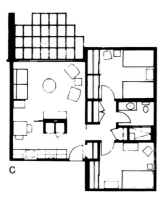

C

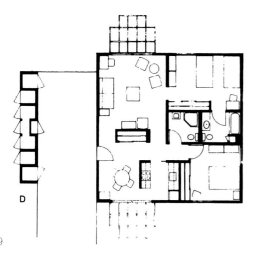

D

Main building, seen across the swimming pool from northeast.

Chapel.

249

Portland Center, Portland, Oregon

The Portland Center rises as a combined residential and commercial district on a site of nearly 83 acres at the fringe of the central business district. It is regarded as one of the most outstanding urban renewal projects in the United States and has already received several awards.

Now occupied are three high-rise apartment blocks, 24 low-rise town houses, a parking garage with a restaurant and a stockbroker's office on the top floor, a shopping center, and three office complexes.

Each of the three apartment blocks stands on a podium which is used as a garage. Their plan is nearly square, with elevators, stairs and refuse shafts placed in the center, surrounded by corridors. Two of the towers have 25 stories, the third has 22. A typical floor contains eight apartments with two to three-and-a-half rooms; on each of the upper floors are four apartments with four to five rooms.

Because the balconies do not extend into continuous galleries, they provide a strong feature of the facades. To ensure privacy and to prevent air drafts, the balconies are flanked to their full depth by the projecting wall panels of the bearing structure.

The low-rise town houses form two clusters of twelve around the two 25-story towers. They are located along the edges of the garage podiums whose landscaped roofs provide access to high-rise and low-rise houses alike. Bedrooms and bathrooms are half-a-story below the entrance while sitting rooms and kitchens are half-a-story above it.

Of the office complexes erected so far, one belongs to the Boise Cascade Corporation and another to the Blue Cross of Oregon. The seven-story main building of the latter is connected by a bridge with a free-standing parking garage where further stories are planned to be added for additional office space.

Outdoor facilities were designed by Lawrence Halprin & Associates, with Charles Moore and William Turnbull as architectural consultants for one of the two parks. In the center is a terrace with two pools of water on different levels, connected by a sprouting cascade.

The apartment blocks, seen from the south. In ▷ the foreground, the lower part of the terrace with the cascade.

Site plan.
1 Apartment block
2 Town houses
3 Terrace with cascade
4 Parking garage, with restaurant and stockbroker's office on the top floor
5 Shopping center
6 General office building
7 Office block of the Boise Cascade Corporation
8 Office block and parking garage of the Blue
  Cross of Oregon

A view of the cascade, looking north. ▷

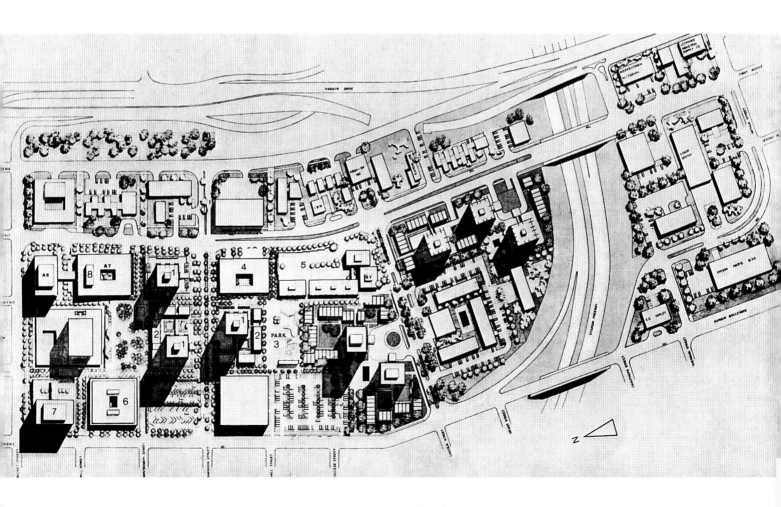

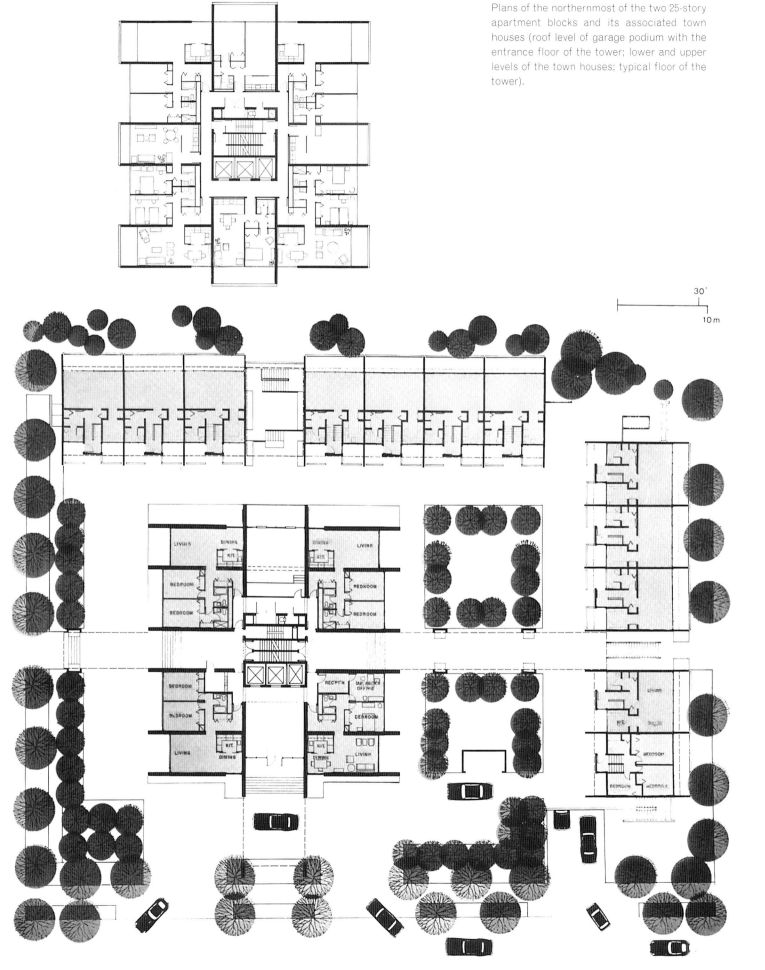

Plans of the northernmost of the two 25-story apartment blocks and its associated town houses (roof level of garage podium with the entrance floor of the tower; lower and upper levels of the town houses; typical floor of the tower).

30'

10 m

As the balconies are not extended into continuous galleries, they provide strong features of the facades.

Access to the town houses is from the landscaped terraces of the garages on which they are erected. Bedrooms and bathrooms are half-a-story below the entrance, sitting room and kitchen half-a-story above it.

Mauna Kea Beach Hotel, Kamuela, Hawaii

The hotel is situated at the northwest coast of Hawaii at the foot of Mauna Kea which rises to 13,796′ above sea level. It was created through the initiative of Laurance S. Rockefeller, who had been asked to support the local efforts to extend the tourist industry vital to the islands.

The complex consists of three buildings, a building with the public rooms in the lower portion and 154 guest rooms in the upper portion, a free-standing dining pavilion, and a buried service wing.

The long main building, asymmetric in relation to the transverse axis marked by the main entrance, stands on the brow of a hill sloping down to the beach. Good use has been made of the topography by placing the public rooms on different levels, the entrance level containing reception lounge and administrative offices is on top, levels with shops, bar and buffet below. The guest rooms are arranged in three stepped-back tiers affording generous space for terraces which are protected by horizontal wooden trelliswork against the sun and against view from above. On the inside, the guest rooms blend with three open-air galleries filled with luxuriant vegetation. The dominant structural feature of the main building is the white-painted poured-in-place concrete, marked at regular intervals with V-shaped linear beads on the surface. The further range of building materials is restricted: Mexican flagstone, Italian quarry tile, local lava and sand-finish plaster.

Within the dining pavilion, the floor level rises in two tiers towards the interior so that all the guests have an unobstructed view of the sea. The inner zone, sheltered by a dark wooden ceiling, has accommodation for 200 diners; many more can be served on the outside terraces. The service block as well as an auditorium which can also be used as a banqueting hall are built into the slope behind the dining pavilion.

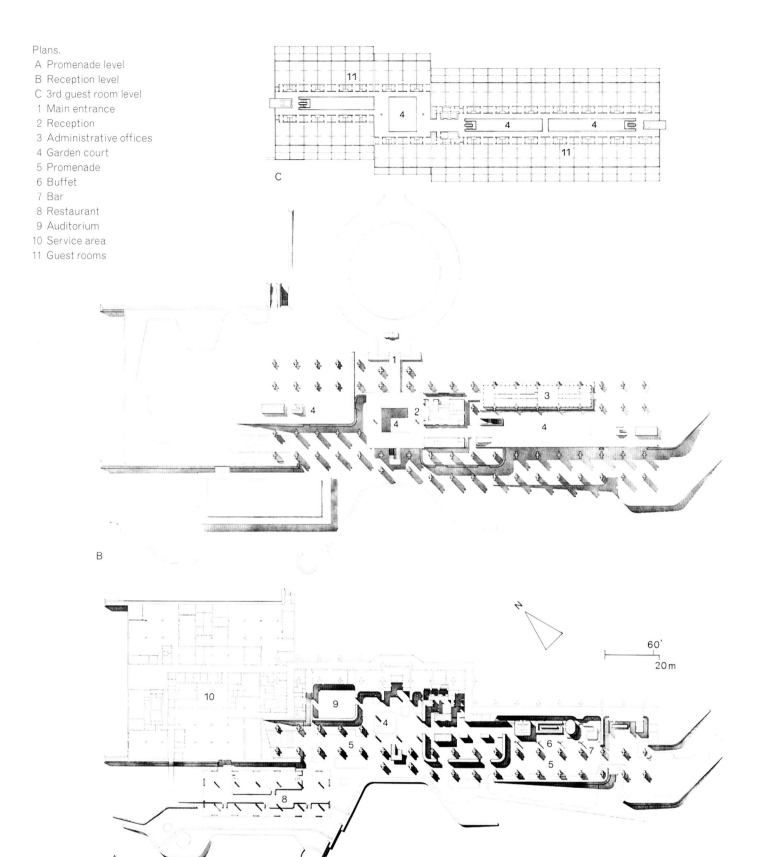

Plans.
 A Promenade level
 B Reception level
 C 3rd guest room level
 1 Main entrance
 2 Reception
 3 Administrative offices
 4 Garden court
 5 Promenade
 6 Buffet
 7 Bar
 8 Restaurant
 9 Auditorium
10 Service area
11 Guest rooms

Entrance zone. The guest room balconies are ▷
protected by horizontally mounted wooden
trelliswork against the sun and against view
from above.

Cross-section.

Side view.

258

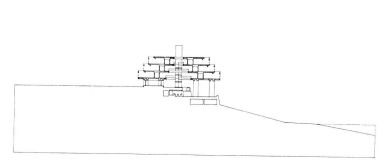

Two-story promenade zone. On the right, on an intermediate level, is the entrance zone.

Garden court at the northwestern end.

Garden court at the southeastern end, seen ▷ from the promenade zone.

Pages 262–263:
General view of the hotel, with the dining pavilion on the left.